The Funniest People in Comedy: 250 Anecdotes

David Bruce

Published by David Bruce, 2022.

While every precaution has been taken in the preparation of this book, the publisher assumes no responsibility for errors or omissions, or for damages resulting from the use of the information contained herein.

THE FUNNIEST PEOPLE IN COMEDY: 250 ANECDOTES

First edition. October 8, 2022.

Copyright © 2022 David Bruce.

ISBN: 979-8215376751

Written by David Bruce.

Table of Contents

Chapter 1: From Actors to Children.......................................1

Chapter 2: From Christmas to Gays and Lesbians.........................12

Chapter 3: From Gifts to Money 24

Chapter 4: From Mothers to Problem-Solving............................37

Chapter 5: From Rehearsals to Yom Kippur 49

Appendix A: Bibliography..60

Appendix B: About the Author 66

Appendix C: Some Books by David Bruce.................................67

Dedication

DEDICATED TO MY SISTER MARTHA

Martha wrote, "When I was working at Longaberger, I worked with a girl who had two children and was in the middle of a divorce. She was so worried about Christmas for her boys. I received a very nice Christmas bonus that year, and I went to my boss and started a donation fund for the girl. My boss told me later that she — my boss —delivered the money to the girl's mother and father and told them not to tell her who brought the money for her. Months later the girl told me that the boys had the best Christmas that year, and she told me someone had brought money to her mom and dad for her, and she went to town and bought the boys Christmas. She never did know who did that for her. She was so thankful. I believe that I was the only one who donated to her, which was just fine."

***

The doing of good deeds is important. As a free person, you can choose to live your life as a good person or as a bad person. To be a good person, do good deeds. To be a bad person, do bad deeds. If you do good deeds, you will become good. If you do bad deeds, you will become bad. To become the person you want to be, act as if you already are that kind of person. Each of us chooses what kind of person we will become. To become a good person, do the things a good person does. To become a bad person, do the things a bad person does. The opportunity to take action to become the kind of person you want to be is yours.

Bai Juyi went to Zen master Daolin of the Tang Dynasty and asked what one must do in order to live in accord with the Tao. Daolin answered, "One must avoid doing evil, and one must do as much good as possible." Bai Juyi was surprised at the simplicity of this answer and said, "Even a child knows that." "True," replied Daolin, "even a child of three knows this but even a man of 80 fails to live up to it."

A seeker after truth once asked a wise person how to seek God. The wise person replied, "The ways to God are as many as there are created beings. But the shortest and easiest is to serve others, not to bother others, and to make others happy."

Cover Photograph for *The Funniest People in Comedy: 250 Anecdotes*

https://pixabay.com/photos/clown-rodeo-cowboy-competition-4991855/

All anecdotes have been retold in my own words to avoid plagiarism.

Anecdotes are usually short humorous stories. Sometimes they are thought-provoking or informative, not amusing.

Chapter 1: From Actors to Children

Actors

• While studying theater at UCLA, Carol Burnett took a course in acting, where she prepared to recite a speech in front of her class. Unfortunately, she didn't recite it very well. For one thing, she didn't bother to read the rest of the play to find out the context of the speech. In addition, she spoke the speech in a low monotone while pantomiming a waitress wiping a table. Her classmates didn't understand the speech and thought that she was pantomiming ironing a shirt. Carol's grade? D minus. Fortunately, a short time afterward, she was given some funny words to say. Her classmates laughed, Carol stuck to funny roles, and she earned an A-minus in the course.[1]

• On *The Dick Van Dyke Show*, Dick's younger brother, Jerry, made a few memorable appearances as Stacie Petrie. One pair of episodes about Stacie's sleepwalking had their genesis in real life. Dick Van Dyke says about Jerry, "As a kid, he was a somnambulist—the world's champion sleepwalker. He could get up, walk, and talk to you, and you'd never know he was asleep." After Jerry was cast for his guest appearance, series producer Carl Reiner asked Dick if his younger brother could act. Dick said yes. When Mr. Reiner asked him how he knew Jerry could act, Dick replied, "Because if he can't, I'll kill him."[2]

• Not everyone wants to act. During the 1970s and 1980s, a wild and crazy comedian named Ron Sweed, aka the Ghoul, hosted several mostly bad movies on a television program airing in Cleveland, Ohio. Frequently, in between segments of the movie he was showing, he did short episodes of "Spencer and Mongolia," a parody of a sitcom. Several women played Mongolia over the years—one woman quit because she regarded filming the episodes as a waste of her lunch hour.[3]

Ad-libs

• Jackie Gleason's TV series *The Honeymooners* was shown live, and mistakes did happen. In one episode, Mr. Gleason, famous for the character Ralph Kramden, missed his entrance. Art Carney, who played sewer worker Ed Norton, simply went to the Kramdens' icebox, took out an orange, and began peeling it until Ralph Kramden arrived. Whenever you see Jackie Gleason patting his stomach on the show, it's a sign to the cast that they're in trouble, and somebody better think of something to say or do to get them out of the jam. Audrey Meadows, in her character of Alice, Ralph's wife, once snarled, "If you get any bigger, Gasbag, you'll float away." The line was an ad-lib, rendered necessary by circumstances.[4]

• Henry Morgan was hired to do a radio program in Canada consisting of ad-libs. However, very quickly, the producer of the show complained that Mr. Morgan was cheating him because the show had no structure—no beginning, middle, or end. So on the next show, Mr. Morgan paused to point out to the audience the beginning of the show, then later he paused to point out the middle of the show, then finally he told the audience, "This is the end—I quit."[5]

• Much of Jack Benny's humor came from his writers, but at least once he got off a funny ad-lib. During a radio show with Fred Allen—who was funny with or without writers—Mr. Allen kept peppering Mr. Benny with comic ad-lib insults. Finally, Mr. Benny protested, "You wouldn't say those things if my writers were here!"[6]

• Vaudeville comedian Ted Healy once came on stage just after a bear act left. The smallest bear left a dropping as it exited, and the amused audience members called for the return of the bear act. Mr. Healy looked at the dropping, then he told the audience, "If that's the kind of crap you want, I'll do it myself." The audience laughed.[7]

• British stand-up comedian Marti Caine once performed her act in front of a group of drunken rugby players immediately after some strippers had performed. A rugby player saw that Ms. Caine was not taking off her clothes, so he yelled, "We want tits!" Ms. Caine replied, "You'd look bright with tits."[8]

• Having dined well at the Trocadero, Robert Benchley strode to the door and asked the doorman to call him a taxi. However, the "doorman" said, "I'm very sorry. I happen to be a rear admiral in the United States Navy." Mr. Benchley replied, "All right, then. Get us a battleship."[9]

• Comedian Beatrice Lillie was dining at a restaurant when a busboy dropped several dishes onto the floor. He started to pick up the pieces, but Ms. Lillie yelled, "Wait for the laugh!" The busboy—and Ms. Lillie—got a laugh.[10]

• While comedian Jebb Fink was performing live, his microphone suddenly sagged in its holder. Mr. Fink got a laugh by ad-libbing, "Oh, the story of my life. It's always going limp when I need it most."[11]

• Wilson Mizner often complained about the apartment where he lived. When his friend, Jim Tully, asked him why he didn't move, he replied, "I can never find my other shoe."[12]

Advertising

• George Burns and Gracie Allen were quite successful at publicity stunts. In 1940, Gracie Allen ran for President on The Surprise Party ticket. She didn't have a candidate for Vice President because she didn't want vice in her administration. During her candidacy, Gracie launched a whistle-stop campaign that ran from Los Angeles, California, to Omaha, Nebraska. Many people are familiar with Pat Paulsen's runs for the Presidency, but Gracie was the first comedian to do this. This was George Burns and Gracie Allen's most successful publicity stunt.[13]

• To advertise its Razzles candy, Mars Candy decided to use a Cleveland, Ohio, show in which comedian Ron Sweed, aka The Ghoul, hosted several mostly bad horror movies. The Ghoul criticized the candy for weeks, and the more he criticized it, the more its sales went up. In gratitude, Mars Candy delivered a case of Razzles to The Ghoul. The case of candy remained on the set of The Ghoul's show for years—unopened.[14]

• Mark Twain understood small print and advertising. One of his advertisements for a lecture tour consisted of the huge words "MAGNIFICENT FIREWORKS" followed by the small print "were in contemplation for this occasion, but the idea has been abandoned." Another of his advertisements read, "The doors open at 7; the trouble begins at 8."[15]

• Peter Cook and Dudley Moore made the film *Bedazzled* (1967), in which the voluptuous Raquel Welch played the sexy role of Miss Lillian Lust. At first, Mr. Cook and Mr. Moore wanted to name the film *Raquel Welch*, so that they could enjoy theater marquees blazing forth this legend: "Peter Cook and Dudley Moore in *Raquel Welch*."[16]

• While working for the Ringling Brothers, comedian Bobby Clark carried a lot of luggage, although many circus performers travel light. When management complained about his excess luggage, Mr. Clark said that he was entitled to it because the circus was advertising him as "bigger and better."[17]

• W.C. Fields wrote the screenplays of many of the movies he appeared in, using such pseudonyms as Mahatma Kane Jeeves or Otis Cribblecoblis. He gave one of his movies the title *Never Give a Sucker an Even Break*, hoping that movie marquees would advertise it as "W.C. Fields—*Sucker*."[18]

Alcohol

• Vaudeville comedian Jim Thornton was an alcoholic. Once, he went on an alcoholic spree with another vaudeville comedian, George C. Davis. Although both men were alcoholics, they were different kinds of alcoholics. Mr. Thornton could stay drunk for weeks, but still keep himself shaved and clean. Mr. Davis, however, let himself go to seed. The two had drunk up all their money, and they needed more money to buy themselves alcohol, so Mr. Thornton asked to borrow $2 from a vaudevillian they met on the street. The vaudevillian refused to lend them anything, so the clean Mr. Thornton turned to the filthy Mr. Davis and said, "George, throw a louse on him."[19]

• Jimmy Durante wanted to confess his sins, so he called Father Bob Perella to come to his apartment, which as usual was filled with Jimmy's friends. When the priest arrived, Jimmy's friend, Fatso Marco, asked the priest what he wanted to drink, then Father Bob and Jimmy went into the bedroom so Jimmy could confess his sins. A few minutes later, the door opened and Fatso brought the priest a drink. Jimmy hollered, "What are you doing? Can't you see I'm making my confession?" Fatso replied, "Just because you got problems, the priest has to go dry?"[20]

• Grantland Rice and humor writer Ring Lardner once shared a hotel suite in Chicago. Mr. Rice was writing articles each day, so he had to work pretty hard. However, Mr. Lardner was writing a weekly column, so he was able to take it easy. For much of the week, Mr. Lardner sat in the hotel suite, drinking and staring at a print on the hotel wall—the print showed a horse-riding competition: the Grand National. At the end of the week, while they were leaving the suite, Mr. Lardner turned to Mr. Rice and said, "Granny, the jock on the second horse isn't even trying."[21]

• Who drummer Keith Moon was one of Monty Python member Graham Chapman's drinking buddies, but he was not always a good friend. Once, Mr. Chapman needed money. As the two were walking, they saw a dustbin filled with garbage. Keith took approximately £2,000 out of his pocket, stuffed it in the bottom of the dustbin, and forced Mr. Chapman to dig through the garbage to get the money.[22]

• When lesbian comedian Judy Carter came out to her mother, she made the mistake of getting drunk first. This meant that she kept stammering and couldn't find the words to tell her mother that she was gay. After hearing a lot of stammering, her mother asked, "Judy, is it you want to tell me you're gay?"[23]

• Deanne Stillman, writer and coeditor of *Titters: The First Collection of Humor by Women*, was once asked where she thought she would be in five years. She replied, "Out to get a beer."[24]

Animals

• At Cornell, practical joker Hugh Troy pulled a notable stunt with the aid of an accomplice. One morning, after a light snow had fallen on the greens of Cornell, Hugh and a friend took a wastepaper basket that had been made out of the foot of a rhinoceros and tied it to the middle of a clothesline so that they were able to lift the foot, then drop it to make a footprint without leaving their own footprints nearby to reveal the practical joke. The next morning, the footprints were discovered, and the zoology professors of the university identified them as belonging to a rhinoceros. The professors followed the footprints to a lake. The footprints continued on the ice of the lake, but disappeared where a gaping hole was in the ice.[25]

• Bob Denver once appeared in a comic Western. In one scene, several very loud blanks were to be fired from a gun held very close to a horse's head. Mr. Denver was worried that the horse would rear up at the noise, but the horse didn't move a muscle. After the scene was over, Mr. Denver asked the wrangler how he had managed to keep the horse so calm. The wrangler motioned to the horse, then said, "Stone deaf."[26]

• In one of Olsen and Johnson's stage successes, Harold Ogden (Chic) Johnson walked on stage carrying a gun (loaded with blanks, of course) which he shot at the roof, after which a chicken fell to the stage and John Sigvard (Ole) Olsen told the audience, "It's a good thing that cows don't fly." Mr. Johnson then shot into the rafters again, and this time a cow fell to the stage.[27]

• Of course, the real star of the television sitcom *Mr. Ed* was Mr. Ed, the horse—not Alan Young, who played Wilbur Post. Because of this, Mr. Young had to do his best in every shot—if the horse was perfect in doing what he was supposed to do, that was the shot that was used. Mr. Young also says that when the horse was tired, that was the end of shooting for the day.[28]

• The family of Quaker humorist Tom Mullen adopted a stray dog, which they named Terry. Terry was so well fed that she was overweight, and because she was overweight, her legs bowed. In addition, her tail wagged so much that one of the Mullen children called her "a story with a happy ending."[29]

• Although many people don't realize it, much wildlife lives in New York City. Comedian (and birder) Bob Smith was watching a motionless Great Blue Heron in a Central Park lily pond when an astonished tourist asked him, "Is it real?"[30]

• While working at WING radio in Dayton, Ohio, comedian Jonathan Winters brought a horse in to be his surprise guest, even though he had to bring it up three flights of stairs.[31]

Audiences
• Harry Houdini used to perform his famous needles-and-thread illusion, during which he seemed to swallow first thread, then sewing needles. After allowing a member of the audience to look into his mouth and verify that no thread and needles were there, Houdini would pull the thread from his mouth, showing the audience that all the needles had been strung on the thread, supposedly while they were in his stomach. During one performance, Groucho Marx was in the audience. When Houdini asked for a volunteer from the audience, Groucho stepped forward and peered into Houdini's mouth. After Houdini asked Groucho what he saw there, Groucho replied, "Gum disease."[32]

• On a horribly cold night in Cleveland, stand-up comedian Judy Carter came out to perform in front of an audience of only two people. She ended up sitting at their table and telling a few jokes. After the "show" was over, the couple invited her to their home for breakfast. She accepted.[33]

• Weird comedian Andy Kaufman once came out on stage and started singing "100 Bottles of Beer on the Wall." The audience hated it, but when Mr. Kaufman left the stage after getting down to "2 Bottles of Beer," the audience wanted him to finish the song.[34]

• Much of Richard Lewis' comedy is about the pain of being alive. One day, some UCLA students—the image of health and happiness—recognized him when he was in his car and shouted to him, "We're in pain, too."[35]

Bombing

• Very early in her career as a stand-up comedian, Carol Siskind bombed horribly in a club in which her brother was a member of the audience. She refused to let him not see her succeed, so she dragged him to another club, where she also bombed. Still refusing to let him go home, she dragged her brother to yet another club, where finally, at 2 a.m., she had a good set. Only after her brother had finally seen her succeed would she let him go home.[36]

• Very early in her career, Phyllis Diller did what all beginning comedians do—bomb. To get into show business, she called the Red Cross and volunteered her services as a comedian. They sent her to a veterans' hospital, where she performed in front of four guys who yelled at her, "Leave us alone—we're already in pain."[37]

• The very dignified Greer Garson guested on Jimmy Durante's program. She didn't know anything about comedy and asked Mr. Durante what would happen if the show wasn't funny. Mr. Durante replied, "Then, Miss Garson, we're all gonna be in the toilet together."[38]

Children

• As a little girl, Sandra Bernhard used to enjoy putting a layer of Elmer's glue on the palm of her hand, letting it dry, then peeling it off—for one thing, the glue had a very nice smell. One day, her father saw her with the glue, and he asked, "Are you sniffing that glue? Well, I sure hope you never sniff airplane glue." Young Sandra responded, "No,

I never would—it can give you brain damage!" This conversation made young Sandra start thinking, and that night, she tried to remember the lyrics of songs from Broadway musicals that she often sang around the house. After a few hours of self-torture, she went to her parents' bedroom and told them that she had brain damage. (She didn't have brain damage, of course.)[39]

• Eddie Cantor was a very popular comedian in early 20th-century America. Being in show business often requires frequent and prolonged absences from home, and after Mr. Cantor had been on an extended tour, he came home late one night and the next morning relaxed in his living room, reading the morning newspaper while waiting for breakfast. His four-year-old daughter came into the living room, saw him, then shouted for her mother, "Mama, mama, come here quick—that man is here again."[40]

• As a child, comedian Cathy Ladman listened over and over to the comedy album *Nichols and May Examine Doctors*, memorizing it, even though she didn't understand all of the album. In fact, after she said her prayers, she would recite part of the album to her mother, who responded by saying, "That's nice, dear"—but who, Ms. Ladman says, must have searched her Doctor Spock book to find out if this kind of behavior in a child was deviant.[41]

• Comedian Jerry Lewis got his first laugh the first time he stepped on stage. When he was a kid, his father, a singer in vaudeville, allowed Jerry to sing, "Brother, Can You Spare a Dime?" At the end of the song, the audience began to applaud. As Jerry was making a bow, his foot slipped and hit a footlight, which exploded, causing the audience to laugh. Jerry decided that he liked the laughter, and so he became a comedian.[42]

• Because of his white hair and large moustache, Mark Twain resembled Melville Fuller, the Chief Justice of the United States. While Mr. Twain was visiting Washington D.C., a little girl saw him, mistook him for Mr. Fuller, and asked, "Mr. Chief Justice Fuller, won't you write something for me in my autograph book?" Mr. Twain agreed, wrote, "It's glorious to be full but it's heavenly to be Fuller," then signed his own name.[43]

• When she was growing up, comedian Margaret Cho worked in her parents' bookstore, which was located in an area heavily populated by gay men. At first, she was scared of them because they dressed in leather and looked tough, even though the worst thing that happened was one of them smiled at her and told her, "I like your purse." As soon as she was old enough to realize that they were gay, she felt safe.[44]

• Groucho Marx's son, Arthur, wanted a BB gun when he was 10 years old. However, Groucho didn't want to get him one, because of the danger, so he said, "As long as I'm the head of the house, you're not going to get a gun!" Arthur replied, "Dad, if I get a gun, you won't be the head of the house!"[45]

• When he was a child, Eddie Cantor served as a waiter to the camp directors of Surprise Lake Camp. He was a very efficient waiter—he never waited for the directors to finish their desserts but would snatch them away half-eaten so he could finish eating them in the kitchen.[46]

• When comedian Sandra Bernhard was a little girl, she decided to see if she could sleep an entire night with a wad of chewing gum in her mouth. Of course, when young Sandra woke up, her mother had to use scissors to cut the gum out of her hair.[47]

• Comedian Tracey Ullman got her first job, helping out at a local bakery, when she was 14. Unfortunately, she didn't last long at the job—whenever she had to put cream cakes into bags, she insisted on licking the excess icing off her fingers.[48]

• As a youngster, comedian Richard Pryor used to perform in school talent shows. His talent for making people laugh made itself known early, and the school auditorium was packed with kids waiting for young Richard to *rehearse*.[49]

• Comedian Beatrice Lillie once wore a $10,000 diamond ring. Child actor Brandon De Wilde looked at it and was properly impressed, saying, "Gosh, I bet that cost $100."[50]

• Jack Benny used to pretend that his car wouldn't start without a kiss. Of course, after his little daughter gave him a kiss, the car started right up.[51]

Chapter 2: From Christmas to Gays and Lesbians

Christmas

• Lou Costello of Abbott and Costello fame really got into Christmas, setting up an elaborate Christmas display each year with angels, music, reindeer, and many hundreds of Christmas lights. Comedian George Gobel lived across the street from Mr. Costello. Mr. Gobel did nothing for Christmas except to put up a sign that said, "See our display across the street."[52]

Clothing

• Some stand-up comedians pay too much attention to what they wear. Comedian Jay Sankey met a comedian who tried to dress in a way that supported his on-stage character (an excellent idea), but who then asked Mr. Sankey what the audience would think of his shoes. Mr. Sankey replied, "If they notice your shoes, you aren't funny."[53]

• Suzanne Rand of the improvisational team Monteith and Rand had a grandmother who bought her incredibly sexy underwear. One day she wore some of the underwear to bed, and when she got up in the middle of the night to go to the bathroom, she looked down and noticed that her crotch was glowing.[54]

• Groucho Marx owned a photograph of a young Harpo Marx. In it, Harpo is wearing mittens and holding a gentleman's leather glove in his hands. Why? According to Groucho, "Harpo heard early in life that a gentleman never appears in public without holding a glove."[55]

• When Carol Burnett was growing up, she lived with her grandmother in a small apartment—so small that young Carol hung her clothes in the shower. For years, whenever Carol put on her clothing, it was slightly damp.[56]

• Beatrice Lillie once dressed in a long formal gown and gave a serious recitation in front of Ethel Barrymore—before lifting her skirt and roller-skating off the stage.[57]

Competition

• Vaudeville comedians often tried to steal laughs from each other. One day, when W.C. Fields was doing his famous pool game routine on stage, Ed Wynn sneaked under the table and began mugging to get laughs. Mr. Fields continued with his act and waited until Mr. Wynn stuck his head out from under the pool table, then swung the cue stick and hit Mr. Wynn hard. The audience thought it was part of the act and howled every time Mr. Wynn moaned. After this incident, Mr. Wynn stopped sneaking under Mr. Fields' pool table.[58]

• Early in Bob Newhart's career, after he had become the hottest comedian in show business, he used to watch the comedians on *The Ed Sullivan Show* to size up the competition. Week after week, he watched the comedians and said, "Well, fella, you're OK, but not socko. We know who's still number one." But after watching a young comedian named Bill Cosby on *Ed Sullivan*, Mr. Newhart said, "Good luck, kid. Take it and run with it awhile."[59]

Contracts

• When comedian/singer Fanny Brice was given a contract by the great theatrical producer Florenz "Flo" Ziegfeld, she wore it out by constantly showing it to her family, friends, acquaintances, and total strangers. Mr. Ziegfeld gave her a new copy of the contract, but when she wore that one out, too, he declined to give her any more written contracts. Ms. Brice kept on working for Mr. Ziegfeld for several years, but their contracts were all verbal, not written.[60]

• Comedian George Burns recognized Jack Haley's talent—Mr. Haley played the Tin Woodsman in *The Wizard of Oz*—and kept introducing him to a producer who ignored him. After Mr. Haley made it big in show business, the producer came up to Mr. Burns and said,

"Why didn't you tell me you knew such a talented guy? I could have put him on contract years ago!"[61]

Costumes

• Benny Hill's relationship with the beautiful women who appeared on his show was professional, although he did form friendships with some of the women—and their husbands. He also listened to their complaints when they had any. For example, one day the actresses on his TV show complained about a costume design that had only a couple of inches of material across the crotch. Colleague Bob Todd told Mr. Hill of the complaints about the costumes, and Mr. Hill—without even looking at the costumes—ordered the wardrobe mistress to change them. According to Mr. Todd, "He was like a Dutch uncle to those girls."[62]

• Famous vaudeville comedian Bobby Clark was seldom recognized unless he was wearing his trademark spectacles—which weren't real spectacles, but were merely drawn onto his face. Even his barber, who had been cutting his hair for years, didn't recognize him. One day, his barber told him that he had seen a comedian with the same name as Mr. Clark on a vaudeville stage and he wondered where the comedian had thought up the crazy things he did. Mr. Clark replied that he had often wondered the same thing.[63]

• In Hollywood, a costumer brought Terry-Thomas his articles of clothing for a scene, dumped them on the floor and said, "These should fit you. I've seen you on TV." Terry-Thomas, known for dressing immaculately, was shocked. "Oh," he said, "so this the way you measure, by looking at people on the TV." He pointed to the shoes. "I told you I needed a size 11. Without trying those on, I can tell you they're a size 8." The costumer replied, "Don't worry. I'll give them a shine."[64]

Death

• Harpo Marx had a very poor education, but the geniuses of the Algonquin Round Table liked him because he was good at games such as croquet. However, he was not so good at the murder game that was sometimes played at critic Alexander Woollcott's house. In the game, a "murderer" would approach the "victim" and give him or her a written message saying that he or she was dead. The victim was supposed to lie down until discovered, and then Woollcott's guests would use their detective skills to discover the murderer. Once, Harpo was the murderer, but the guests realized that immediately because Harpo's written message to his victim was, "You are ded."[65]

• Buster Keaton's movie masterpiece *Steamboat Bill Jr.*, contains a memorable gag. A hurricane blows the front of a house over on top of Buster, and he escapes unharmed only because he is standing in the exact spot where he will be safe—the spot where the house has an open window. The gag was carefully planned: Buster had exactly three inches of clearance over his head and beside each shoulder. The front of the house weighed two tons (it had to be built that heavy so that it wouldn't twist in the wind created for the movie), and if it had actually hit Buster, it would have killed him instantly.[66]

• While serving as a soldier in World War II, Spike Mulligan knew an eccentric soldier who occasionally went AWOL for a few weeks, then turned himself in. The eccentric soldier was sent to see a military psychiatrist, to whom he complained about being made to wear a uniform. The psychiatrist asked why he didn't like the uniform, and the eccentric soldier explained, "It's dangerous. Germans shoot at it on sight." The psychiatrist's report stated, "There is nothing wrong with this man. He has a wholesome fear of being shot by Germans."[67]

• In 1928, when comedian Henry Morgan was thirteen years old, he and a few friends went to Palisades Park on the first day the amusement park opened for the season. While they were there, a man offered them a free ride on the roller coaster. Afterward, young Henry, who admits that he was a nosy kid, asked the man why he had let them ride free on the roller coaster. "Oh, it's the beginning of the season," the man explained. "We wanted to see if it's still safe."[68]

• Groucho Marx was dragged to see a medium by his wife. He was reluctant to go because he didn't believe the medium could communicate with the dead, but he perked up when he heard that the medium would answer any question asked of her. Groucho's question was, "What's the capital of North Dakota?" The medium didn't know the answer, and two of her muscular male confederates threw Groucho out of the séance.[69]

• Marie Dressler was a silent movie comedian who worked with Charlie Chaplin. During World War I, she was so famous that some American G.I.s stationed in France named a cow after her. When the cow was killed during the war, newspaper headlines stated, "'MARIE DRESSLER' KILLED IN LINE OF DUTY," and the real Marie Dressler had a hard time convincing other people that she hadn't died.[70]

• During World War I, French silent film comedian Max Linder fought against the Germans. At the First Battle of the Aisne, Mr. Linder was machine-gunned. The Germans thought he was dead, and they sent a message of condolence to Mr. Linder's film company. Fortunately, Mr. Linder survived.[71]

• When comedy writer Barney Dean was in a hospital dying of cancer, Bob Hope visited him. Mr. Hope wondered whether Mr. Dean knew that he was going to die, just as Al "Jolie" Jolsen had died a few weeks earlier. When Mr. Hope walked into Mr. Dean's hospital room, Mr. Dean asked, "Got any messages for Jolie?"[72]

• Monty Python member Graham Chapman was always late for everything. After Mr. Chapman died, fellow Python member Michael Palin joked at the funeral, "I'd like to think he's with us now—well, at least he *will* be in 20 minutes."[73]

• Henny Youngman's most famous one-liner was, "Take my wife—please!" At his funeral, Rabbi Noach Valley of the Actors' Temple in New York prayed, "Dear God, take Henny Youngman—please."[74]

Education

• As a comedian with cerebral palsy, which affects her control of her muscles, Geri Jewell has been in some interesting situations. When she showed up to take her driving test, the examiner refused to allow her to take it on the grounds that she was drunk! And when she went on a field trip to a psychiatric hospital with her college psychology class, one of the attendants thought she belonged there. When she tried to leave with the rest of the class, the attendant told her, "Come on now, honey. You can't go with those people. This is your home here." Ms. Jewell had to yell for help so her professor could tell the attendant that she was a student—the attendant was shocked and muttered, "I guess they're letting *everybody* into college nowadays."[75]

• When his two sons were attending UCLA, comedian Joe E. Brown was invited to join his sons' fraternity—provided that he become an undergraduate. Mr. Brown paid the tuition and even attended a physics class, where he challenged the professor's statements and even asserted that Albert Einstein had called him for advice. (This was a somewhat true statement, but of course Mr. Einstein hadn't called Mr. Brown for advice about physics.) After the class was over, the professor told Mr. Brown, "Stay away from my class, and I'll give you an A, but if you ever show your face in here again, I'll flunk you."[76]

• Before W.C. Fields left for Australia on a vaudeville tour, he had a bookseller fill a large trunk with classic books. Australia in those days had little to offer in the way of entertainment, and sea voyages to Australia took a long time, so the books were a necessity. Mr. Fields, by the way, became a great fan of Charles Dickens, and apparently was influenced by Dickens' comedy. It's impossible for many people to read the words of Mr. Micawber in *David Copperfield* without hearing those words being spoken by Mr. Fields.[77]

• Gay comedian Bob Smith eagerly read through the J.R.R. Tolkien Middle Earth books in the 10th grade, ignoring his homework for a while, and even reading the books in class. Teachers never became angry at him for reading in class, but they would say, "Excuse me, Bob," a few times to get his attention, then add something such as, "I know that an English teacher should encourage reading ... but, Bob, would you mind putting your book away?"[78]

• When comedian Kate Clinton was a teacher, she bored her class by teaching them how to make plurals of nouns—mouse/mice, etc.—something that annoyed them because an exception seemed to exist for every rule. Finally, she asked one youngster, "Steve, spell the plural of leaf." He looked at her, then answered, "T-R-E-E."[79]

• A recent fad is to collect the high-school yearbooks of famous people. Anyone who collects comedian Robin Williams' yearbook won't be surprised to see his name listed in a column of students thought to be "Most Humorous," but they may be surprised to see his name listed in the column of students thought to be "Least Likely to Succeed."[80]

Food

• Celebrities have an advantage over other people in that they can get into crowded restaurants quickly by mentioning their name. While Groucho Marx and his family were waiting in line to get into a crowded restaurant, his wife asked him to let the headwaiter know who he was so they would be seated quickly. (This was in the days before Groucho grew a real mustache, and so he had not been recognized.) Groucho didn't want to reveal his name because he didn't like the kind of restaurants that catered to celebrities. In fact, Groucho had given the headwaiter a fake name: Sam Jackson. However, his wife was persistent, so finally he tapped the headwaiter on the shoulder and said, "My wife wants me to tell you who I am. My name's not really Jackson. It's Abe Schwartz, and I'm in the wholesale plumbing business. And this is Mrs. Schwartz, and all the little Schwartzes."[81]

• Will Rogers had a little son named Jimmy who loved cake—lots of cake. Jimmy was invited to a party, and his parents cautioned him to take only one piece of cake, and he promised to obey. After the party, they asked how many pieces of cake he had eaten, and he said just one, adding that the hostess had wanted him to eat more than one piece: "Mrs. Jones kept pushing it at me, and I kept saying, 'No,' and I don't think she liked it. She said, 'Why, Jimmy, everybody likes my cake!'" Finally little Jimmy had found a way to keep her from tempting him with more cake: "I thought of what Dad says sometimes, so I told her, 'You just better take that damn stuff out of here.'"[82]

• Comedian Jay Leno grew up in a working-class family, and he declines to pay excessive prices for food, despite being a multi-millionaire. When he was a struggling comedian in New York, he used to eat at the Stage Deli, where he would buy a hamburger for $1.10, because he didn't want to spend $4.50 for a roast beef sandwich. After becoming hugely successful, he took his wife, Mavis, to the Stage Deli, where he planned on finally eating a roast beef sandwich. However, the price had changed—the roast beef sandwich was now $9.50. Mr. Leno said, "I'm not paying $9.50! It used to be only $4.50! I didn't want it *that* much."[83]

• As starving comedians very early in their career, Richard "Cheech" Marin and Tommy Chong had to come up with creative ways to get food. Cheech used to write letters to the companies that marketed food he liked and tell them that he had found something gross in their food—even though he hadn't. For example, he would write a famous soup company and tell them that he had found flies in their soup. The companies almost always responded by sending him cases of free food. Once, a company vice president even personally delivered three expensive steaks to him.[84]

• Selma Diamond was one of the earliest women to make her living from writing comedy—she wrote for such comedians as Jimmy Durante, Milton Berle, and Jack Paar. For years, she lived in New York, but eventually she left to write comedy in Hollywood. After being gone for nine years and becoming a big success, she returned to New York and went into the candy store she used to frequent. She asked the owner, "Did you know where I've been?" He replied, "You been buyin' your candy from the store across the street?"[85]

• When he was growing up, Sam Levenson and his friends occasionally headed for Central Park to go hiking. While there, the kids got hungry, but fortunately their mothers always packed their lunches. Each time the kids went hiking, the "miracle of the sandwiches" took place: One of the children would say he was tired of the sandwiches his mother fixed for him, the other children would agree, so everybody would swap sandwiches. But miraculously, all the kids ended up with salami sandwiches.[86]

• Lisa Kron performs a theatrical one-person show titled *101 Humiliating Stories*. One of the stories is about her walking down the hall in a law office, stopping along the way and talking to everyone she met. Once she is down the hall, a female employee tells her, "Your skirt is tucked into your tights." Ms. Kron says she felt like telling everyone in the law office, "You don't get a butt like this eating Slim-Fast for lunch. You have to eat a real lunch to get a butt like this."[87]

• For a while, Joan Rivers told many, many fat jokes about Elizabeth Taylor—for example, "She puts mayonnaise on an aspirin" and "Her car has a bumper sticker that says, 'My other car is a refrigerator.'" Ms. Taylor was a good sport and sent Ms. Rivers word that the fat jokes did not offend her—in fact, the fat jokes had inspired her to lose weight.[88]

• One of Red Skelton's most famous comedy routines demonstrated the different ways in which people dunk donuts. While doing this routine, Red ate as many as eight or nine donuts. When you consider that in vaudeville, a comic might do a routine five times a day, it's easy to see why Red's physician ordered him to stop doing the routine.[89]

• When comedian Dick Gregory was in high school, he wanted to learn etiquette. So he took a high-school cooking course, where he learned not to eat all the meat, then turn the plate and eat all the potato, then turn the plate and eat all the greens.[90]

• Comedian Eddie Cantor's wife wanted him to eat his spinach, which he disliked, so she used to hide it under his mashed potatoes.[91]

Friends

• Early in his career as a stand-up comedian, Jay Leno worked in a lot of strip clubs. One club was the Teddy Bear Lounge in Boston. The strippers weren't hookers; they were working-class women who worked hard to earn a good living. They also were very supportive of Mr. Leno, who was working in a place notoriously difficult to get laughs. One day, he was doing his act in front of two naked women taking bubble baths in tubs that looked like giant champagne glasses. The crowd was not interested in Mr. Leno's act, and a man in the audience started heckling him. One of the women got out of her giant champagne glass, walked over to the heckler, grabbed him by his collar, and punched him in the face, giving him a bloody nose. Then she walked back to her bubble bath. Mr. Leno says today, "That was the first time in my life that a nude woman had to defend my honor."[92]

• Jimmy Durante was a very gregarious fellow. Wherever he had a hotel suite, it was constantly filled with his friends—and with his friends' friends. One day, the telephone rang, and the hotel operator told Jimmy that Dave Rappaport from New Jersey wanted to see him. Jimmy didn't know any Dave Rappaport from New Jersey, so he asked the numerous people in his suite if they knew a Dave Rappaport from New Jersey. It turned out that they didn't know him, either. "So nobody ever hoid of him," Jimmy said. "Ah, what the hell, tell him to come on up anyway."[93]

• While the members of Monty Python were filming their movie *The Life of Brian*, Ian Johnson made a documentary of the process, during which he asked the various Pythons to comment on each other. They got together in a group to watch the documentary, in which they had been open about each other, including criticisms of each other, but after seeing the documentary, a moment occurred during which they all looked at each other as if to say, "Yes, I know you. I know your good points, your bad points, but the hell with all that anyway, because—I *like* you."[94]

• After becoming famous as an entertainer, Will Rogers was occasionally seen doing his comedy act by people from back home. One person saw Mr. Rogers' act, then he returned home where friends asked him what Mr. Rogers was doing to become so famous. He replied, "Oh, just acting the fool like he used to do around here."[95]

• Jack Benny used to fall down on the floor laughing at the witticisms of his friend George Burns. In his later years, whenever Mr. Benny saw Mr. Burns coming, he would say, "Wait, let me lie down on the floor. I'm too old to fall."[96]

Gays and Lesbians

• The homes of gay men tend to be cleaner (and better decorated) than the homes of many single straight men and lesbians. Lesbian humorist Ellen Orleans once visited the home of a gay friend of hers. While talking to her, his roommate, another gay man, moved a vase and saw a ring. He immediately got a bottle of Windex, sprayed the ring, and wiped it clean, all without stopping his conversation with her. Meanwhile, her friend prepared himself a bowl of oatmeal, spilled two flakes on the floor, and immediately got a Dustbuster and cleaned up the flakes. He noticed Ms. Orleans staring with disbelief at him and his roommate, and he said, "We can't help it. We're gay."[97]

• A talent manager—one of the top people in the field—told gay comedian Bob Smith early in his career that he could go far if only he would drop his gay material. Despite making only $3,000 a year from his comedy back then, Mr. Smith was not tempted to accept the advice.[98]

• Lesbian humorist Ellen Orleans remembers her very first gay bumper sticker: "I'm One Too." As she was driving on the highway, a car filled with women pulled up beside her. The women rolled their windows down and shouted, "So are we!"[99]

• After coming out as a lesbian for the first time to her audience, stand-up comedian Judy Carter had a good set and the audience gave her a standing ovation. She started crying because the audience had accepted her for who she was.[100]

• Whenever people ask lesbian humorist Ellen Orleans what the Bible says about homosexuality, she says that the last time she checked, it said, "Love thy neighbor."[101]

Chapter 3: From Gifts to Money

Gifts

• Early in the careers of country comedy duo Homer and Jethro, work (and pay) was hard to get, and consequently, food was hard to get. During this period of poverty, Jethro had a birthday, and Homer bought him a present with the little bit of money he had—a hot dog and a Coke. The birthday present was much appreciated.[102]

• When Jewish comedian Myron Cohen bought a farm, his friend Bill Robbins brought him a house-warming present—a cow. Mr. Robbins said, "She's a real Holstein. But to make her feel more comfortable, maybe we'd better change her name to Goldstein."[103]

• Gay men tend to like comedian Margaret Cho. One gay man sent her a beautiful basket of Vidal Sassoon hair care products, which pleased her until she realized that all of the products were for dry and damaged hair. Ms. Cho says, "Thanks, bitch."[104]

Husbands and Wives

• One of Fanny Brice's three husbands was Nicky Arnstein, a small-time con man. Mr. Arnstein was a talker: a person who was always going to make it big, but who got most of his money from rich women. Still, he was handsome, and he understood the good things in life—that is, the good things in life that are expensive. Eventually, he spent time in prison after being convicted of masterminding a bond robbery. Fanny stayed true to Nicky while he was in prison, even naming her and Nicky's second child after Nicky's lawyer. Fanny never believed Nicky was involved in the bond robbery; she once told the press, "Mastermind? He couldn't mastermind an electric bulb into a socket."[105]

• Margaret Dumont played a high-society woman who was the target of Groucho Marx's amorous (and money-grubbing) affections in 12 years of films by the Marx Brothers. Once, a reporter—influenced perhaps by the many marriage proposals Groucho made to Ms. Dumont on screen—wrote that the two were married in real life. When Ms. Dumont told Groucho that the reporter's mistake was embarrassing, he replied, "Embarrassing? I've just written a magazine article about my wife, and the magazine is printing her picture. When the article comes out, I'll be arrested for bigamy."[106]

• Comedian Rita Rudner got married in a courthouse, and she and her husband didn't spend a lot of money on wedding photographs. Instead, both of them brought cameras. She asked a passerby to take their photo, so her wedding photo shows her and her husband smiling, and in the background are a soft drink machine and a man drinking a Diet Coke. However, it could have been worse, and it was. Her husband's camera contained a very old roll of film, and when it was developed, in addition to the one wedding photo, she saw lots of photos of her husband's old girlfriends.[107]

• Zero Mostel's relationship with his second wife, Kate, was sometimes stormy. Once, they decided to separate. Kate was in bed, turned away from her husband, while Mr. Mostel thundered around the room, packing his suitcase. Finally, he said, "Aren't you going to turn around and say good-bye?" She did, and saw Zero standing by the bed holding a suitcase and dressed only in his hat, socks, and shoes. She laughed and told him to come to bed.[108]

• Charlie Chaplin and Jim Tully were walking in Hollywood on a side street when they came across a wedding party. The group recognized Mr. Chaplin and asked if he would mind having his photograph taken with the bride and groom. He consented, and after the photo was taken, started walking again with Mr. Tully. For a while, the much-married Mr. Chaplin walked with his head down, then he said, "Poor devils."[109]

• Goodman Ace was a comedian of the 1950s who had his own highly successful radio show and worked as a writer on Milton Berle's TV show. He knew many of the famous comedians of his day. While walking with Groucho Marx in New York, the two passed a wedding. Groucho, who had been divorced twice, tapped the bride on her shoulder and said softly, "I tried it twice—it's no good."[110]

• As a Valentine's Day surprise for his wife, Nell, comedian Garry Moore hired a skywriter to create this message in the sky: "GARRY LOVES NELL." (One of his presents to her was a belt with rivets spelling out the rather crowded words "MY NAME IS NELL I AM A MARRIED LADY BUT THANK YOU JUST THE SAME.")[111]

• Natalie Schafer, who played Mrs. Thurston Howell on *Gilligan's Island*, kept her age strictly a secret. (When she died in 1990, she was 90 years old.) When her husband, Louis Calhern, was on his deathbed, he asked her to reveal her age to him. She looked her dying husband straight in the eyes and replied, "Never!"[112]

• After seeing Elizabeth Taylor appear on television wearing her new, huge diamond given to her by her husband, Richard Burton, comedian Zero Mostel told his friends, "I wanted to buy that diamond for Kate [his wife], but that son-of-a-bitch Burton outbid me by $50."[113]

• Comedian Rita Rudner bought a massage for her husband as a birthday gift. Big mistake. The doorbell rang, Rita answered it, and a beautiful, blonde, 18-year-old woman said, "I'm here to give your husband a massage." Ms. Rudner replied, "He's dead."[114]

• When Gracie Allen was young, she had a crush on Charlie Chaplin. Once, she met him—and he even kissed her on the cheek! Whenever George Burns would ask her to say something funny, Gracie replied, "Charlie Chaplin."[115]

• Movie director Billy Wilder had a strange sense of humor. While he was in Paris, his wife asked him to buy a bidet. He was unable to buy one, so he wired his wife, "Unable obtain bidet. Suggest handstand in shower."[116]

• Redd Foxx married a beautiful but small-talented singer. After one of her concerts, she asked him, "How'd I sound tonight?" Mr. Foxx replied, "Honey, you hit a note tonight that curdled the drinks."[117]

• In 1954, comedian Ernie Kovacs married singer Edie Adams. The marriage vows were in Spanish—which neither the groom nor the bride understood.[118]

Illnesses and Injuries

• While serving as a soldier in World War II, Spike Milligan knew a young soldier named Sergeant Cusak, who became the first in the group to get crabs. Sergeant Cusak went to Piccadilly to fill a prescription for blue unction—whose only function is to treat crabs. Not wanting to be embarrassed, he whispered to the pharmacist, "Can I have some blue unction?" Unfortunately, the pharmacist asked loudly, "BLUE UNCTION?" Knowing that everyone had heard the pharmacist, Sergeant Cusak replied loudly, "YES, I'VE GOT BLOODY CRABS!"[119]

• Movie actor Christopher Reeve's life changed on May 27, 1995. While competing in an equestrian event, he broke his neck and was totally paralyzed. In October of that year, a Russian doctor entered his room and started making insane comments. Mr. Reeve recognized the Russian doctor as an old friend—comedian Robin Williams—and he started laughing. Mr. Reeve says about the visit, "I knew I was going to be all right." Well, maybe not totally all right—Mr. Williams was pretending to be a Russian proctologist.[120]

• When Jack Benny was ill, he had to get shots in his backside twice a week. His nurse gave him his shots in alternate cheeks, but sometimes she had trouble remembering which cheek should receive the next shot. So finally Mr. Benny walked into the doctor's office, dropped his pants, and on one cheek was printed "Tues" and on the other, "Thurs."[121]

• David Letterman gets some of his ideas for his material from such publications as the *National Enquirer*. For one story, the *Enquirer* used this headline: "How to Lose Weight Without Diet or Exercise." Mr. Letterman thought logically and realized, "That leaves disease."[122]

Insults

• Comedian Joey Adams appeared many times on *The Ed Sullivan Show*, which was famous for scheduling a wide variety of acts—musical, comic, juggling, animal, whatever. For one appearance, Mr. Adams had to share his dressing room with a performing chimpanzee. However, Mr. Sullivan stopped by the dressing room to apologize: "I'm sorry we had to put you two together." Mr. Adams replied, "That's all right," and Mr. Sullivan joked, "I wasn't talking to you."[123]

• Comedian Joan Rivers tells a true story about the worst date in her life. Years before she became famous, she had a blind date with a student who was attending Yale. The blind date arrived, looked at Joan, turned to the person who had arranged the blind date, and said, "Why didn't you tell me?" Then he walked away, leaving Joan and her friend behind.[124]

• Groucho Marx got on an elevator that was carrying actress Greta Garbo, who was wearing a hat. Playfully, he lifted up the back of her hat and tilted it over her face. This made Ms. Garbo angry, and she said, "How dare you!" Groucho apologized: "I beg your pardon. I thought you were a fellow I knew from Kansas City."[125]

Language

• W.C. Fields had many famous friends, including Will Rogers, a comedian from Oklahoma who was known for his folksy accent and humor. However, Mr. Fields occasionally made jokes at his friends' expense. One day, after Will Rogers had visited him in the hospital, and the nurse was raving about how wonderful Will Rogers was, Mr. Fields said, "The son of a bitch is a fake. I'll bet a hundred dollars he talks just like everybody else when he gets home."[126]

• Tim Allen, popular star of the TV sitcom *Home Improvement*, spent time in prison for drug dealing. (He admits that dealing drugs was "stupid.") Today, he tells about a Colombian drug dealer who was put in a prison cell with an American bank robber. The Colombian couldn't speak English, so the bank robber taught him English, starting with the sentences "Don't touch the alarm" and "Put the money in the bag."[127]

• When Quaker humorist Tom Mullen and his wife, Nancy, toured Japan, a Japanese airline steward told them not to stay at a certain hotel, saying, "This hotel is a sort of rest house for an instant couple." And Mr. Mullen once saw a detour sign written in both Japanese and English. The English said, "Danger. Drive sideways."[128]

• In vaudeville and on TV, the comic material of Red Skelton was kept scrupulously clean. When Mr. Skelton was in Nashville, Tennessee, he was asked why no four-letter words were in his performances. Mr. Skelton replied, "Why should people pay me to say words they can read for free on the bathroom wall?"[129]

Letters

• Comedian Lisa Geduldig is both Jewish and a lesbian. For her, family interaction is important. While doing her act, she sometimes reads a letter from her parents. In it, they express sympathy about a recent breakup of her romantic relationship—and they try to set her up with a nice Jewish woman. However, to be honest, her parents didn't write the letter. Ms. Geduldig grew tired of receiving emotionless letters from her parents, so whenever she writes them, she also writes the reply she would like to receive from them. She sends her parents the emotion-filled reply along with her letter and asks them to sign it and mail it back to her.[130]

• Some people can't distinguish between a comic persona and a real person. According to his radio show, comedian Jack Benny paid his valet Rochester only $12 a week. This upset a lawyer in Cleveland so much that he wrote several letters to Mr. Benny, complaining about his cheapness. In real life, of course, Mr. Benny was very generous, and Eddie "Rochester" Anderson was paid thousands of dollars per week for his performance in Mr. Benny's half-hour radio program. Mr. Benny was finally forced to write the lawyer and ask him to stop sending those foolish letters.[131]

• Jimmy Durante used to close his performances by saying, "Good night, Mrs. Calabash—wherever you are." Frequently, people would write him letters asking who Mrs. Calabash was; Mr. Durante always wrote back, "Thank you for your letter about Mrs. Calabash. I'd like to tell you about her, but there are some things a gentleman doesn't talk about."[132]

Mishaps

• Shemp Howard was a member of the Three Stooges for 10 years after Curly had a stroke in 1946. While shooting the short *Brideless Groom*, an actress was supposed to slap Shemp around, but she was afraid she would hurt him and so she pulled her punches way too much. Shemp pleaded with her to really let him have it—and she did, giving Shemp a long series of hard slaps and finally knocking him through a door. Afterward, she tearfully apologized to a groggy Shemp, who replied, "It's all right, Honey. I said you should cut loose, and you did. You sure as hell did."[133]

• The family of Donald O'Connor performed in vaudeville and traveled in a car with all of their costumes, tumbling mats, and other stage paraphernalia. One day, a little smoke started coming from the car. Someone yelled "Fire!"—and people grabbed axes and fire extinguishers from their office buildings and, Mr. O'Connor says, "literally beat our act to death."[134]

• Silent-film comedian Ben Turpin, who was famous for his crossed eyes, saved his money and had a happy retirement. When he was an old man, he enjoyed directing rush-hour traffic in downtown Los Angeles. With his crossed eyes and wildly swinging arms, he always managed to royally screw up traffic.[135]

Money

• Country comedian Jerry Clower knew a very religious general store owner named Duvall Scott who recites a Bible verse every time he opens the cash register drawer to put money in. For example, if a child buys a piece of candy, Mr. Scott will open the cash register drawer and say, "Suffer the little children to come unto me." If a son comes in to buy something for his father, then Mr. Scott will open the cash register drawer and say, "Honor thy father and mother." One day, a city fellow driving a big car and pulling a fancy horse trailer came in to buy a horse blanket. Mr. Scott went to the back of the store, brought back a blanket and said, "That'll be $5." The city fellow said, "This is a real expensive horse. I don't put any $5 blankets on him," so Mr. Scott went to the back of the store and looked over his stock. All he had was one kind of horse blanket in different colors, so he put the blanket down, picked up another blanket of a different color, brought it to the front of the store, and said, "That'll be $25." The city fellow said, "My horse is famous—too famous for a $25 blanket. Do you have anything better?" Mr. Scott went to the back of the store again, picked up yet another blanket in yet another color, brought it to the front of the store, and said, "That'll be $50." This time, the city fellow was satisfied, and he cheerfully handed over the $50, then walked out of the store. Of course, the other people in the store knew what was going on, and they wondered which Bible verse Mr. Scott would quote. Mr. Scott put the money in the drawer, and he said, "He was a stranger, and I took him in."[136]

• Many famous, rich people grew up poor, and their early poverty affected how they regarded money. Comedian Fred Allen once paid $300 to rent a cottage in Maine for the summer. (Obviously, this was a long time ago.) After the money had exchanged hands, a syndicate offered Mr. Allen $2,000 a week to write a column every other day. However, he turned it down. His friend Groucho Marx asked him why, and Mr. Allen explained, "I paid $300 for that cottage up in Maine, and if I accept this job I'll have to stay in New York. I'd be out the $300." So the syndicate raised its offer—to $3,000 a week. But Mr. Allen again turned the syndicate down. Groucho was incredulous, and he told Mr. Allen, "Why don't you forget about the $300? You could take one week's salary from the syndicate and own that cottage outright." Mr. Allen replied, "I paid $300 to live in that cottage this summer, and that landlord is not going to get my money for nothing!"[137]

• Walter Catlett made a good living playing eccentrics in movies of the 1930s through the 1950s. (He played the comic Sheriff in the screwball comedy *Bringing Up Baby*, which starred Cary Grant and Katherine Hepburn.) Mr. Catlett was also an eccentric in real life. One day, he ran out of money playing roulette at Agua Caliente, a gambling house in Mexico, so he pulled out his false teeth and bet them. He won and collected the price of the dentures: $350. He was well known for his drinking ability and his propensity to spend his money on having fun. When the stock market crashed in 1929, he thought it was hilarious that everyone else was as broke as he was, without having had the fun of spending their money. Yet another reason why he was so often broke was that he gave much of his money away to charity and the needy.[138]

• At age 15, comedian Rita Rudner wanted to be a dancer, so she moved to New York City to study dancing. However, at age 15, she did not understand the intricacies of tipping. Once, she ordered and ate a turkey sandwich, then left without tipping. The waiter came running after her on the sidewalk and told her, "You forgot to leave me a tip." She handed him her wallet and told him, "Take what you want—just don't hurt me." The waiter took $5 from her wallet, saying, "That's one dollar for serving you the turkey sandwich and four dollars for making me run down the street." Even at age 15, Rita was a comedian, so she said, "Why don't you take two dollars for serving me the sandwich and three dollars for running down the street?"[139]

• Comedian Jerry Lewis once boasted about a one iron he owned that he said was the best ever made. Pro golfer Sam Snead heard the boast, and he invited Mr. Lewis to try his one iron. Mr. Lewis tried it, hit the ball further than with his own one iron, then attempted to buy the one iron from Mr. Snead. On hearing the first offer—$100—Mr. Snead said, "No, no." On hearing the second offer—$200—Mr. Snead said, "No, losing that club would ruin my whole bag." On hearing the third offer—$500—Mr. Snead said, "Run with it before I change my mind," and so Mr. Lewis handed over the money and took off running across the golf course.[140]

• Before becoming rich (but not before developing his habit of overtipping), Jackie Gleason overtipped himself into poverty at a hotel. Without enough money to pay his bill, he decided to walk out on his hotel bill. He put on every article of clothing he owned, covered himself with a robe, then walked out, telling the hotel management that he was going for a swim. A year later, he was in funds again and returned to the hotel to pay his bill. He walked up to the hotel owner at the front desk, and the owner shouted, "Oh, my God! We thought you had drowned!"[141]

• When comic singer Anna Russell decided to sell her house in Australia and move back to the United States, she decided to get rid of many of her possessions. Many items were auctioned off, but an assortment of odds and ends were dumped into her living room, where she held a farewell party and rummage sale. Her maid looked at the stuff, then asked, "Why don't you give the garbageman an extra $10 to cart it away?" Fortunately, Ms. Russell did not listen to the advice, because at the rummage sale she made over $900.[142]

• Early in her career, stand-up comedian Judy Tenuta used to make money on the side insulting people at parties. For example, a woman would pay Ms. Tenuta to go to her house and insult her husband on his birthday. At the birthday party, Ms. Tenuta would say such things as, "Hi, it's your birthday, pig. Come, let me play my accordion in your face." A fringe benefit of these performances was free food. Ms. Tenuta would always ask that food be brought to her so she could eat as she insulted the guest of honor.[143]

• The Marx Brothers flopped in London with a vaudeville skit called "On the Mezzanine." During the skit, the Londoners began to throw pennies on the stage—a deadly insult. Groucho went to the front of the stage, raised his hand for silence, then said, "If you people are going to throw coins, I wish to hell you'd throw something more substantial—like shillings or guineas." This joke was quoted throughout London, and the Marx Brothers became successful in London with a different skit titled "Home Again."[144]

• To gain experience as a comedian very early in his stand-up career, Jay Leno used to go into a bar and ask the manager if he could do his act. If the manager said, "Get out of here," Mr. Leno would whip out a $50 bill and say, "Just let me tell some jokes, and if people leave or I embarrass the customers, you can keep the fifty." All the managers returned his money to him, and a few invited him back to perform again—and next time they let him pass the hat.[145]

• Comedian Richard Pryor grew angry at the low wages paid by Budd Friedman, owner of the Improv comedy club, so he confronted Mr. Friedman and accused him of paying him less because he was black. Mr. Friedman denied the charge, and later, he told his wife what Mr. Pryor had said. She replied, "You should have told him that you take advantage of all performers, regardless of race, color, or creed." Despite the confrontation, the two men remained friends.[146]

• Zero Mostel got involved in show business as a result of some gallery talks on art he gave at the Museum of Modern Art. Always a comedian, he spiced up his talks by making his audience roar with laughter. Because of the word-of-mouth reputation he received, he soon was asked to entertain at parties, where he received $3 or $5—he also asked for "all the pastrami sandwiches" he could eat.[147]

• Very early in her career, Carol Burnett worked in the Catskill Mountains. A voice coach named Ken Welch heard her, was impressed, and wanted to teach her. Unfortunately, Ms. Burnett had very little money. Mr. Welch offered to teach her for free until she got a better-paying theater job, but Ms. Burnett gave him IOUs, which she paid off with quarters she earned as a hat-check girl.[148]

• Stand-up comedian Judy Carter believes in rewarding the laughing members of her audience. Back when she performed in small clubs, if only a few members of the audience laughed at one of her jokes, she would take money out of her wallet, go over to the laughers, and hand them the money. This always got the audience's attention and greatly encouraged laughter.[149]

• Comedian Bill Dana grew up in poverty. Often, he, his siblings, and his parents were forced to hide from bill collectors. While the family sat in a room with drawn curtains and a locked door, the bill collector would bang on the door and shout, "I know you're in there." Someone in the family would always softly say, "We know we're in here, too."[150]

• Perhaps the wealthiest Monty Python member is hard-working John Cleese. A British newspaper once called several celebrities to see what they would do if they won £1 million in a competition. Among the celebrities they called was Python member Graham Chapman, who said, "I would give it to John Cleese so he could take the afternoon off."[151]

• Back when magicians Penn Jillette and Teller (this single name is now his legal name) were performing on the streets, Penn very effectively convinced members of the audience to give generously after a show by telling them, "Remember: I'm six-six, I have three very sharp knives, and I have an excellent memory."[152]

• As a young comedian, Lily Tomlin created a sensation at the Improv by arriving in a chauffeur-driven limousine. Actually, she didn't have much money. The chauffeur had been parked in the theater district, waiting until a play was over. Lily paid him $5 to take her to the Improv.[153]

• Fanny Brice was a huge star who made thousands of dollars a week. George S. Kaufman and Moss Hart told her that they would write a play for her if she would agree to be paid $1,000 a week. She declined, saying, "If I take $1,000 a week, everybody in America will be writing plays for me."[154]

• Wilson Mizner came from a good family who supplied many diplomats to America, but he hung around with lowlifes. One day, a friend who was a burglar asked him for a loan of $50. Mr. Mizner gave it to him, but asked, "What's the matter—doesn't it get dark anymore?"[155]

• In the 1960s TV series *Get Smart*, enemy agents continually tried to assassinate Control agent Maxwell Smart. The constant bombings, shootings, and knife attacks on Max perplexed Max's landlord—until Max told him that he worked for the Internal Revenue Service.[156]

• Ben Turpin was a silent-film comedian who was amazed at his own success, including financial success; he often walked into public places and introduced himself by saying, "Ben Turpin! Three thousand dollars a week!"[157]

• Some charity benefits don't make money. Comedian Eddie Cantor once showed a committee how to save $500—by not holding the benefit at all![158]

Chapter 4: From Mothers to Problem-Solving

Mothers

• Jewish comedian Sam Levenson grew up in a very poor household. Gas was expensive and definitely not to be wasted. Therefore, before leaving the house en masse for any length of time, the family always turned the gas off. One day, they forgot. After the family returned home from a visit, Mr. Levenson's Mama noticed that the boiler was steaming. Immediately, she barked two orders: "Somebody shut off the gas!" and "Everybody into the bathtub!"[159]

• In the late 1880s, a young woman had her fortune told by a gypsy, who said to her, "You will marry and have a son known all over the world." The young woman did marry, and one of her sons was Larry Fine, who became a member of the world-famous comedy team known as the Three Stooges. Whenever Larry's mother went to see a Three Stooges short comedy film at the cinema, she would shout, "That's my son!"[160]

• Country comedian Jerry Clower grew up in an impoverished family in rural Mississippi. When he was a youngster, his mother used to fix fried chicken, then tell her children to save the chicken back and neck and feet for her, as they were her favorite parts. When he grew up, of course, Mr. Clower realized that his mother loved her children and she wanted them to eat the best parts of the chicken.[161]

• When Nancy Cartwright, the voice of TV's Bart Simpson, was pregnant with her first child, she kept telling her midsection, "Please don't be Bart! Please don't be Bart!"[162]

Music

• Country comedian Jerry Clower sometimes toured with country singer Mel Tillis, and they had a wonderful relationship. Mr. Clower would come out first to start the show, then Mr. Tillis would come out with his act. Always, Mr. Tillis would say before the last song of the night, "Ladies and gentlemen, let's get the nation's number-one country comic back out here on stage and let you applaud him again." Then Mr. Tillis would invite Mr. Clower to stay on stage and sing the last song with the band.[163]

• The comedy team of Laurel and Hardy was greatly loved throughout the world. In 1953, after Stan Laurel and Oliver Hardy had stopped making movies, they went on tour in the British Isles. When their boat came to Cobh, Ireland, the pier was lined with hundreds of Laurel and Hardy fans. As the boat docked, all the church bells in the city started ringing out Laurel and Hardy's movie theme song. Both Laurel and Hardy cried.[164]

• Entertaining in the days of radio could be interesting. English comic singer Anna Russell had an Aunt Bena who invited her neighbors over to listen to opera on the radio. All of her guests dressed up in formal evening clothes, and they sat in chairs arranged in rows just like they were at the opera. During intermission, they drank champagne.[165]

Names

• In Beverly Hills, Terry-Thomas was walking (something not often done in Beverly Hills) and noticed that each street was lined with a different variety of tree. Wondering about the name of an unfamiliar species, he stopped and asked a Mexican gardener, "I wonder if you could tell me what this is?" The gardener stopped working, stared at Terry-Thomas, then answered scornfully, "It's a tree."[166]

• Robert Benchley invited writer J. Bryan III, who was from Virginia, to dinner, saying that he had invited a female companion for him. At the dinner, he introduced Mr. Bryan to a Chinese woman. "This is Miss Ching Lee," Mr. Benchley said. "I invited her for you because you're from Virginia, and everybody from Virginia is related to the Lees."[167]

People with Handicaps

• When comedian Geri Jewell, whose muscle control is affected by her cerebral palsy, tried to get into a college psychology class with a door that was locked because the class was already filled with students, she first knocked on the door and then accidentally fell down some stairs. The students inside the classroom had been watching, and one informed the professor, "There's some drunk girl out there who just fell down the stairs." After a quick trip to the nurse's office, Ms. Jewell again approached the psychology professor. He opened the door, looked her over, then said, "If you kids are going to take every drug on earth, why bother to come to school at all?" (After he understood the real situation, the professor became one of Ms. Jewell's friends.)[168]

• Jonathan Winters was a very funny comedian who has suffered from mental illness. Once, he parked in a handicapped parking space, and a woman protested, "You're not handicapped." Mr. Winters looked at her and said, "Lady, can you see into my mind?"[169]

Police

• Shortly before he had to go on stage, Groucho Marx took his new car out for a spin. Unfortunately, he didn't realize that the traffic at that time of day would be so heavy, and he found it difficult to make it back to the theater on time for his cue. In desperation, he made an illegal turn and was stopped by a policeman. Groucho attempted to explain the situation, but the policeman didn't believe him and said, "If you're one of the Marx Brothers, let's hear you say something funny." Groucho snapped back, "If you're a policeman, let's see you arrest somebody." The policeman laughed, then gave Groucho an escort to the theater.[170]

• Ellen DeGeneres says that being pulled over by the police makes her nervous, so she tries to lessen the tension by making jokes. One day, she was pulled over for speeding. When the police officer asked if she knew why she had been pulled over, she replied, "Because of the dead bodies in the trunk?" (The police officer was not amused.)[171]

• Comedy writer Barney Dean was taking a walk in Beverly Hills—a place where people almost never walk, preferring instead to have their chauffeur drive them wherever they want to go. Suspicious, a motorcycle police officer stopped him, and Mr. Dean asked, "How fast was I going, officer?"[172]

Politics

• Harpo Marx had a servant who did many kinds of work for him, including serving as his chauffeur. This man did not wear a uniform, and he wandered freely around the grounds, pausing to watch Harpo's guests play croquet or tennis. One day, one of Harpo's guests was Herbert Bayard Swope, who as a politician prided himself on being able to remember names and faces. Mr. Swope looked at Harpo's servant, knew that he had seen him somewhere before, but could not remember his name or where he had seen him. After a long struggle with his memory, Mr. Swope finally gave up, went over to the man, and said, "Good afternoon. I'm Herbert Bayard Swope." The reply came back, "Pleased to meet you. I'm Benny Murphy, Harpo's chauffeur."[173]

• Comedian Joy Behar once announced on her radio show that next time she would read "a list of 10 reasons why Rush Limbaugh couldn't get laid." Her bosses advised her not to read the list on her radio show, so it became a First Amendment issue. She didn't read the list on the air, but she explained that she was being censored, thus creating more controversy than if she had read the list. Of course, the next time she performed at a club, fans called for the list, and she read it to them. What about her radio show? Ratings went up, but she was fired anyway.[174]

• Comedian Kate Clinton lives in Provincetown, Rhode Island. In 1992, her next-door neighbor, Peter, asked if she had heard the terrible fight the night before. She hadn't, so Peter told her how bad the fight had been, with people yelling "f—ing liar and f—ing this and that" at each other. Suddenly, Ms. Clinton realized what had happened, and she said, "Oh, Peter! We were watching the Republican convention, screaming at George Bush in his speech. We had the windows open. Sorry." Peter replied, "I agree, dahlin.'"[175]

Practical Jokes

• Impressionist Rich Little played a practical joke on Bette Davis. At the urging of a friend, he called her up, imitated the voice of her friend Jimmy Stewart, and succeeded in fooling her for a while, until she asked a question that Mr. Little did not know the answer to, but Mr. Stewart would have. Ms. Davis did not take the joke well. She demanded to speak to the person who had put Mr. Little up to the joke, and she told that person, "I'll never have anything to do with you or Rich Little again!" Later that evening, Mr. Little saw both Jimmy Stewart and President Ronald Reagan, and he told them the story of the practical joke. President Reagan knew Ms. Davis, and he offered to call her to patch things up. He called her, said, "Hello, Bette. This is Ronald Reagan," then a moment later, he hung up the telephone. Asked what had happened, President Reagan related, "She said, 'F—k you, Rich Little!' and hung up."[176]

• Tim Conway used to hang out with some friends in a projection room at a television station in Cleveland, Ohio. At night, the telephone switchboard was closed, so the calls were routed into the projection room. Mr. Conway sometimes pretended to be an answering machine. He would answer the phone and say, "When you hear the tone, leave your name, number, and message." But then he would beep before the caller had finished talking and say, "No, you didn't say it fast enough. You have to get your message in between the tones. Now try it again." Again, he would beep before the caller had finished talking. Callers would try to talk faster and faster until they finally realized that they were the victims of a practical joke.[177]

• Mark Twain was at the races outside London, where he met a friend who had lost all his pocket money gambling and who asked if Mr. Twain would buy him a ticket back to London. "I'm nearly broke myself, but I'll tell you what I'll do," Mr. Twain replied. "You can ride under my seat, and I'll hide you with my legs." The friend agreed, but unknown to the friend, Mr. Twain bought two train tickets. When the train inspector came by to collect the tickets, Mr. Twain handed him the two tickets, then said, "My friend is a little eccentric and likes to ride under the seat."[178]

• As a teenager growing up in Indianapolis, Indiana, David Letterman worked in a grocery store. One day, he was ordered to stack up cans in a display. He did stack the cans—all the way to the ceiling, using an arrangement in which if a customer removed one can, the entire stack of cans would fall down. On another occasion, he got on the intercom and announced a fire drill. The customers left the store, and not all the customers laughed when they discovered that the fire drill was a hoax.[179]

• When Sheldon Leonard co-starred with Bud Abbott and Lou Costello in *Abbott and Costello Meet the Invisible Man*, a dialogue coach made his life miserable, insisting that he was performing the dialogue incorrectly no matter how he said it. After some time, when Mr. Leonard was ready to kill the dialogue coach, Mr. Costello revealed that it was a practical joke—the dialogue coach was just an actor he and his partner had hired to plague him.[180]

• Humorist Robert Benchley invited Frank Case, the manager of the Algonquin Hotel, to dinner, and when Mr. Case arrived, he discovered that almost everything in Mr. Benchley's home had come from the Algonquin Hotel—the towels, the soap, the tableware, the napkins, everything bore the insignia of the Algonquin Hotel. (Mr. Benchley had secretly arranged with Mr. Case's staff to borrow a bunch of Algonquin stuff for the dinner.)[181]

• When famous movie stars Charlie Chaplin and Mary Pickford were walking together in Hollywood, they would occasionally be recognized and crowds of fans would follow them. Because the movies back then were silent, none of these fans had ever heard them speak. To amuse themselves and astonish the fans, Mr. Chaplin and Ms. Pickford sometimes spoke to each other using high, squeaky voices.[182]

• Practical joker Hugh Troy used to give dinner parties at which he served oysters on the half shell. Frequently, one of the guests found a pearl and Mr. Troy congratulated the guest. Unfortunately, when the guest visited the jewelry store the next day to get the pearl appraised, the guest would discover that the "pearl" had been purchased at a five- and ten-cent store.[183]

• David Brenner is funny in real life. Once, he was riding on a crowded subway. The only available seat was stained, so he put his newspaper on the seat, then sat down. A man asked, "Are you reading that newspaper?" Mr. Brenner replied, "Yes," then stood up, turned the page, and sat down on the newspaper again.[184]

• Sydney Smith was both a clergyman and a wit. Once, a lady guest at his country estate suggested that the estate would be more beautiful if it had deer. When the lady woke up the following morning and looked out her window, she saw two donkeys with deer antlers tied to their heads.[185]

• Harpo Marx and Oscar Levant were motoring on Long Island when Harpo drove alongside another car, then pointed West and asked, "Denver?"[186]

Prejudice

• At the Atlanta airport, country comedian Jerry Clower saw a little white boy trip and gash his head. Blood was flowing freely, the boy's mother was upset, and airline employees were calling for help. A good-looking, well-dressed black man stepped up to Mr. Clower and said, "Mr. Clower, I am a medical doctor. Would you ask the mother if it would be all right for me to check the little boy?" Mr. Clower understood why the black doctor had spoken to him first—if the doctor had been white, the doctor would have spoken to the mother directly. Mr. Clower did speak to the mother, the mother gave permission for the black doctor to attend to her boy, and when emergency personnel arrived, they said nothing more needed to be done because the black doctor had already done everything excellently. Mr. Clower writes, "I hope one day we grow to the point where an individual can perform as a professional, whatever his race, nationality, or origin."[187]

• When African-American comedian Dick Gregory first went into show business, he worried about how to react when some yahoo screamed racial epithets at him. For six months he had his wife scream insults at him while he figured out the best way to react. Finally, he asked his wife, "What would you do if from this day on I started referring to you as 'bitch'?" She replied, "I'd just ignore you." Mr. Gregory was impressed by the attitude with which she said that, and he used that attitude in his act. Later, he found comic ways to respond to racial insults. When someone called him "nigger," he replied very politely, "According to my contract, the management pays me $50 every time someone calls me that. Please do it again."[188]

• In the Jim Crow era, black comedian Nipsey Russell engaged in this bit of socially relevant material. Blacks who attempted to vote in the South were often given a literacy test that involved many questions and was impossible to pass. In one bit Mr. Russell told, a would-be black voter was asked, "What did the Founding Fathers mean when they said all men were created equal?" The would-be black voter, realizing that he would not be allowed to vote no matter what he answered, replied, "They meant when you're white, you're right; when you're brown, you could stick around; but when you're black, get waaaay back!"[189]

• In his act, black comedian Dick Gregory used to tell a story about being in a restaurant down South during Jim Crow days. The white waitress told him, "We don't serve colored people here." Mr. Gregory replied, "That's all right, I don't eat colored people. Bring me a whole fried chicken." Just then, three members of the KKK walked in and told Mr. Gregory, "Boy, watch what you do, because whatever you do to that chicken, we're going to do to you." So Mr. Gregory picked up the chicken and *kissed* it![190]

• Comedian Bob Smith's parents accepted his homosexuality. His father, a retired state trooper, once attended an Annual Policemen's Ball where some men sitting with him and his wife (Sue) began to talk about "fags." His father said, "You know, my son's gay. And it takes a lot more guts for him to deal with being gay than it does for jerks like you to sit there talking with your mouths full and your heads empty. And I don't have to listen to it. C'mon, Sue. Let's sit somewhere else."[191]

• As a Jewish comedian, Groucho Marx endured anti-Semitism—and mocked it. One summer, he tried to join a beach club so that his son could enjoy the water. However, the manager of the club told him, "We don't allow Jews to swim at our beach." Groucho replied, "What about my son? He's only half-Jewish. Would it be all right if he went into the water up to his knees?"[192]

• When comedian Bob Smith's grandmother found out that a family she was friends with would be kept out of her country club because they were Jewish, she protested by inviting every Jewish friend she had to a luncheon at the country club. Eventually, through the efforts of Mr. Smith's grandfather, the Jewish friends became members of the country club.[193]

• In Ocean City, Maryland, stand-up comedian Steve Mittleman walked out on stage to do his act. A man in the audience yelled, "You look Jewish." Mr. Mittleman replied, "You look prejudiced."[194]

Problem-Solving

• As a teenager, Jay Leno got a job at a Ford saleslot doing odds and ends. Among his jobs was taking the hubcaps off the cars at night so they wouldn't be stolen and putting them back on the next day. One day, as he was carrying the hubcaps, he met the new sales manager, a man who made him so nervous that he dropped the hubcaps. This made the new sales manager furious. He yelled at Jay, "This is the Ford Motor Company. You can't treat our property this way! You're fired!

Get out!" Jay was ashamed to lose his job, so after thinking for a couple of days, he wrote the top guy—Henry Ford II in Detroit—asking for his job back. Soon, Jay's old boss called him and said, "I don't know who the hell you know in Detroit, but if you want your old job back, come on back here."[195]

• Jackie Gleason's big spending habits in his adult life may have something to do with his extreme poverty while growing up in New York City. His father left him and his mother, and the two had a rough time trying to survive. In 1952, after Mr. Gleason had become successful in show business, a friend walked into Jackie's bedroom and saw him packing a steamer trunk with clothes that had been wrapped around stacks of dollar bills in different denominations. When the friend asked him what he was doing, Jackie said, "I have been poor before in my life. Right now, I'm rich. So I'm packing a cash nest egg in this trunk, and I'm sending it to a warehouse with a 'will call' on it in case I ever need it."[196]

• Lesbian humorist Ellen Orleans ran into a problem when she acquired her Honda Accord. She is short, and she had trouble reaching the pedals—even after she had moved the seat as far forward as it would go. Therefore, she took the car to her mechanic to see how much it would cost to extend the floor tracks of the seat so she could move it further forward. How much? Too much! Fortunately, her car mechanic is highly intelligent, and he solved the problem in an original manner. He simply bolted a hockey puck to each of the pedals—gas, brake, and clutch. Now Ms. Orleans can comfortably and safely reach the pedals.[197]

• In 1977, Brett Butler was reading water meters in Alabama. To escape the monotony of that boring job, she enlisted in the Bulldozer Repair Division of the United States Army. However, on the very first day of duty, she changed her mind and informed her recruiting officer that she wanted out of the Army. He declined, saying, "We own your sorry *ss." The recruiting officer's attitude made Ms. Butler perform with grace under fire. "Look," she said, "if I have to fly a hammer-and-sickle flag, stick a needle in my arm, and start eating p—sy, I will!" She was discharged—and quickly.[198]

• Gracie Allen could make a stand when a stand was necessary. A dry cleaner ruined a dress that she had taken to him, but he refused to pay for the dress. That evening, in the middle of the vaudeville act she performed with her husband, George Burns, she told the audience about the dry-cleaning incident and recommended that they not patronize that particular establishment, then she went on with the act. The next day, the dry cleaner paid her the money for the dress he had ruined.[199]

• Impressionist/comedian George Kirby wanted a job with Count Basie. Therefore, Mr. Kirby went to a concert by Count Basie and his orchestra. Count Basie used to sit at a piano, plink a note and have his drummer enter, plink another note and have another band member enter, and so on until the entire band was on stage. Mr. Kirby, without authorization, walked on stage, and impersonated Count Basie to the audience's delight. Count Basie also enjoyed the joke, and he hired Mr. Kirby.[200]

• Jackie Gleason was known for drinking heavily. A friend locked up his liquor cabinet to keep Mr. Gleason from getting loaded, but when he came home, he discovered that Mr. Gleason was drunk. Remarkably, even though the liquor cabinet was still locked, the booze containers were empty. (Mr. Gleason had used a screwdriver to remove the back of the liquor cabinet. After drinking the liquor, he screwed the back of the cabinet on again.)[201]

• Rags Ragland played big, dumb guys in forties movies. While he was working in burlesque, a young comic kept trying too hard to get laughs and steal the scene from him, so Mr. Ragland warned the comic to stop stepping on his lines or he would nail him to the floor. The young comic ignored him, so Mr. Ragland got a hammer and nails and nailed the soles of the comic's shoes to the floor, then left him on stage as the other acts performed.[202]

• British comedian Benny Hill suffered from stage fright, so when he had to appear live, he often carried a heavy book to keep his hands from shaking.[203]

Chapter 5: From Rehearsals to Yom Kippur

Rehearsals

• Jimmy Durante and Carol Channing rehearsed and rehearsed a comedy scene for his show. Finally, a bystander interrupted them and said, "What are you still rehearsing for? Both of you know the scene. I think maybe you're just a little nervous." Mr. Durante simply smiled at Ms. Channing and said, "Ah, the confidence of the amateur."[204]

• Jackie Gleason and Milton Berle spent decades making people laugh. After Mr. Berle had guested on Mr. Gleason's TV show, Mr. Gleason said, "We did good, Milton," and Mr. Berle replied, "We did good, Jackie." Then Mr. Gleason said, "How could we be bad? I've been rehearsing for 35 years—and you 50."[205]

Revenge

• Once an older comic asked comedian Henny Youngman to give him some jokes, saying he would pay him for the jokes later that evening. Mr. Youngman agreed, gave him the jokes, and showed up for their rendezvous later that day. The older comic drove up in his fancy car, but ignored Mr. Youngman, leaving him unpaid on the pavement while the older comic went inside a fancy restaurant to dine with his friends. However, Mr. Youngman was able to get revenge. He saw some sign painters working nearby, so he told them that he was almost broke and had decided to sell his car. He then hired them to paint "For Sale—$25" on the older comic's fancy car.[206]

• Some sexist comedians make jokes about forcing their girlfriends to sleep on the "wet spot" following sex. Canadian comedian Meg Soper responds by saying that if her boyfriend ever tries to make her sleep on the wet spot, she is going to give him no further opportunities to make wet spots.[207]

• It wasn't smart to mess with silent film comedian Mabel Normand. She once got into a major argument with movie executive Abraham Lehr, so she backed him into a corner, sprayed him with her perfume, then told his wife that she had seen him leaving a high-class, very expensive cathouse.[208]

• When Joan Rivers broke up with an early boyfriend who was working on a Ph.D., she invented an interesting way of getting revenge. She scattered the pages of his doctoral dissertation all over the floor—the pages were unnumbered.[209]

Signs

• Jimmy Durante opened a nightclub with a few friends as investors. Because they were low on funds, they bargained for a low price from a signmaker. The bargaining worked. Instead of paying $350 for the sign, they paid only $250. Unfortunately, when the sign was delivered, it read: "CLUB DURANT." Mr. Durante protested to the signmaker, but the signmaker said adding the extra E would cost $100, so the club opened with a misspelled name.[210]

• Comedian Bob Newhart put up a sign saying "Armed Dog" at his Bel-Air house. Many people look at the sign and don't even realize it's funny because they are so used to seeing signs that say "Attack Dog" and "Armed Guard on Duty."[211]

Straight Men

• Fred Allen, a funny man, played straight man early in his career. One show, he got off a funny ad-lib that the audience enjoyed very much, but which the comedian he worked with did not. The comedian was furious, and he talked to Mr. Allen in the dressing room after the show. While still carrying a toilet plunger for a cane and wearing a light bulb for a nose, slap shoes on his feet, and a mangy fur coat with big patches on it around his shoulders, the comedian told Mr. Allen, "I'll be goddamned if I play straight for anybody."[212]

• Believe it or not, Oliver Hardy regarded himself as a straight man for Stan Laurel. In addition to his modesty, Mr. Hardy was unselfish when it came to comedy. Once, a gag had been given to his character, but he pointed out that the gag fitted Mr. Laurel's character better, and so the laugh was given to Mr. Laurel.[213]

Telegrams

• Henny Youngman was having lunch with Jerry Lewis one day when Mr. Lewis, a very hot comedy star, was mobbed by fans asking for his autograph. Because Mr. Lewis was so busy signing autographs, he was unable to pay attention to Mr. Youngman. Therefore, Mr. Youngman was able to leave the table, go to the lobby of the hotel and order that a telegram be sent to Mr. Lewis, then return back to the table—all without Mr. Lewis noticing that he had been gone. When the telegram arrived, Mr. Lewis read: "Dear Jerry. Please pass the salt. Henny."[214]

• Natalie Schafer, the actress who played Mrs. Thurston Howell in *Gilligan's Island*, did the pilot episode primarily to get a free trip to Hawaii, never dreaming that a TV network would actually pick up the series. One day, she received a telegram and starting crying. Because Ms. Schafer's mother had been ill, her friends crowded around and offered sympathy. Ms. Schafer had to explain that her mother had not died: "No, no, no—the series sold!"[215]

• Charles Lindbergh became an international hero as the result of a solo flight across the Atlantic. A few days after Mr. Lindbergh had triumphantly landed in LeBourget in France and made headlines throughout the United States and Europe, humorist Robert Benchley sent a telegram to Charles Brackett in Paris: "Lindbergh left here week ago. Am worried." Mr. Brackett cabled back: "Do you mean George Lindbergh?"[216]

• A cigarette company once wanted to advertise on a radio series that would star humorist Robert Benchley. They wired him: "What do you smoke?" Mr. Benchley didn't want to do the radio series, so he wired back: "Marijuana."[217]

• In 1948, many people thought that Thomas Dewey would easily defeat Harry S. Truman in the Presidential election. After the election was over, and Mr. Truman had won, Bob Hope sent this telegram to Mr. Dewey: "Unpack."[218]

Telephones

• Dick Van Dyke was a fan of Laurel and Hardy, and he was eager to visit Mr. Laurel after he (Mr. Van Dyke) had arrived in California. After a year of unsuccessfully trying to get Mr. Laurel's telephone number, Mr. Van Dyke finally found it—in a telephone book: "Stan Laurel, Ocean Avenue, Santa Monica." Mr. Laurel was truly a nice man: he answered fan mail, and he received visitors in his apartment—Mr. Laurel had his telephone number listed so that his fans could find him.[219]

• Carl Reiner left the series *The Dick Van Dyke Show* to appear in the feature film *The Russians Are Coming, The Russians Are Coming*. Taking over his duties as producer were Bill Persky and Sam Denoff. One day, the telephone rang and Mr. Persky answered it. A voice asked, "Is this Carl Reiner?" He answered, "No, but I'm doing the best I can."[220]

• Jack Benny's comic persona was cheap. One day, Mr. Benny made a long-distance, person-to-person telephone call to his agent, Milt Josefsberg, but the telephone operator told his agent, "Person to person to Mr. Milt Josefsberg from Mr. Jack Benny, only I don't think it's really him because he didn't call collect."[221]

Television

• According to Alan Young, one of the good guys of show business was Ted Knight, who starred as Ted Baxter on *The Mary Tyler Moore Show*. (Mr. Young, of course, played Wilbur Post on the TV sitcom *Mr. Ed*, which featured a talking horse.) The two actors crossed paths early in Mr. Knight's career. Mr. Ed used to be driven to the set of his series in a horse trailer that had "Hello, I'm Mr. Ed!" painted on both sides. Often, Mr. Young would be driving to work at the same time and would form a procession with the horse trailer. Of course, other motorists would recognize Mr. Ed and Mr. Young, and they would honk and wave. One day, one of these motorists was Mr. Knight, then a character actor newly arrived in Hollywood, who was driving with his kids in the car. Mr. Knight and the kids waved to Mr. Young, and Mr. Young waved back. In his autobiography, *Mr. Ed and Me*, Mr. Young writes about later meeting Mr. Knight, "Ted said he felt that the reassuring sight of their TV friends, Wilbur and Ed, driving merrily along made them feel at home and welcome in their surroundings."[222]

• The lagoon filmed in the TV series *Gilligan's Island* was artificial—and after a while the water got funky. One day, the crew of *Gilligan's Island* released a live trout in the water—five minutes later, it floated to the surface, dead. Seeing that, Bob Denver, who played Gilligan, said, "If the trout can't live in that water, I'm not going in it." The studio executives didn't want to pay the money to drain and refill the lagoon, so Mr. Denver offered to go in the lagoon if one of the studio executives went in first. The lagoon was drained and refilled.[223]

• Early in his career, Buck Henry, the co-creator (with Mel Brooks) of the TV series *Get Smart*, appeared on television talk shows as G. Clifford Prout, who argued with a straight face that naked animals were an affront to decency and that we must either start clothing our animals or face moral decay.[224]

• Bill Cosby stood up for the integrity of his sitcom *Cosby*. His TV son, Theo, had an anti-apartheid sticker on his bedroom door. NBC wanted to remove it, but Mr. Cosby threatened to quit. NBC backed down.[225]

Theater

• The comedy team John Sigvard (Ole) Olsen and Harold Ogden (Chic) Johnson were famous in the 1930s and 1940s for their no-holds-barred comedy performances. At the beginning of each performance of Olsen and Johnson's stage show *Hellzapoppin'*, a man walked through the audience carrying a small plant and yelling, "Mr. Jones!" Periodically throughout the performance the man would appear walking in the aisles and yelling for Mr. Jones, and each time the man appeared, the plant he was holding was bigger. At the end of the show, when the audience walked through the lobby, they saw the man sitting on a branch of a big tree in the lobby, still yelling, "Mr. Jones!"[226]

• Jack Benny was capable of great enthusiasm. In 1956, he attended a revue titled *For Amusement Only* in London, and he laughed and laughed. Unfortunately, he was the only one laughing. The actors thought a wise guy or a drunk was in the audience, and they asked the theater manager to talk to him during the intermission. After a few minutes, the manager returned and, awe-struck, said, "It's Jack Benny. He *loves* the show." In fact, Mr. Benny loved the show so much that he saw it more than once, and he made sure that VIPs such as Sam Goldwyn, Van Johnson, and Tyrone Power also saw it.[227]

• Whoopi Goldberg can be controversial. One of her theatrical sketches features a teenage girl who gives herself an abortion. Many people were upset by this sketch and picketed the theater where she was performing, but Ms. Goldberg declined to stop performing it. Instead, she thanked the picketers for giving her lots of free publicity.[228]

• When magicians Penn and Teller won an Obie, their theatrical show was so unusual that the presenters of the award didn't know what to call it. Therefore, they officially gave the award to Penn and Teller for "whatever it is they do."[229]

Tobacco

• Comedians Paul Rodriguez and Elaine Boosler were getting ready to perform in a prison when guards came by with a prisoner in shackles. Mr. Rodriguez picked up Ms. Boosler and carried her over to the prisoner and asked, "Hey, man, how many cigarettes will you give me for her?" The prisoner replied, "No offense, but I don't like women anymore; however, I'll give you a carton if *you'll* spend the night with me."[230]

• Comedian Joe Cook used to hang 26 "No Smoking" signs in 13 different languages in his dressing room—but he didn't mind if his visitors smoked.[231]

Work

• During the Joe McCarthy era, people were scared of Communists and of anyone who was politically to the left of boring—uh, center. Zero Mostel was called to testify before the House UnAmerican Activities Committee. The blacklist had hit Hollywood, and Zero was no longer being offered work by Twentieth Century-Fox. When Zero was asked if he had ever been in Hollywood before 1942 to work in his profession, he replied, "Oh, yes, I was signed to a contract with Twentieth Century-Fox—or was it Eighteenth Century-Fox?" Another thing Zero did was to point to the Committee chair and say in a loud stage whisper, "That man is a schmuck," but this was deleted from the official record of his testimony.[232]

• Comedian Jay Sankey learned quickly that a stand-up comedian does five minutes when the comic is supposed to do five minutes, 20 minutes when the comic is supposed to do 20 minutes, and an hour when the comic is supposed to do an hour. In fact, comedy clubs have a red light that flashes on and off to let the comic know it's time to wrap up the set. One night, he didn't see the red light come on, so he was startled when the speakers boomed out with the sound man's voice, saying, "This is the voice of God! Get off the stage!" Mr. Sankey ran off the stage—and bought a wristwatch.[233]

• Buddy and Vilma Ebsen were a brother-and-sister dance act whose first big break came when they danced in the chorus of Eddie Cantor's hit show *Whoopie*. They rehearsed on stage, but to rehearse they had to use the work lights. This expense upset some people, and in Chicago they weren't allowed to use the work lights to rehearse. However, the star of *Whoopie*, Eddie Cantor, found out about it, so he had this sign posted: "If any youngsters are ambitious enough to practice every day in order to get out of the chorus, I will pay for the work lights. Eddie Cantor."[234]

• For a while, comedian Tim Conway worked in Cleveland television, but often he would commute to Los Angeles and get work there. Eventually, he was offered a part in the TV sitcom *McHale's Navy*, starring Ernest Borgnine. He was uncertain about whether to accept the job offer, but his Cleveland boss made the decision for him, saying, "You're fired. If you don't go out [to Hollywood], you're nuts. So you're fired." Mr. Conway went to Hollywood and became a star.[235]

• When Danny Thomas was an unknown entertainer with a wife and a daughter (Marlo), he felt pressured to take a job as a grocery clerk. So he went into a church and prayed to St. Jude (the patron saint of lost causes) for a sign about what he should do. Within a week, he was a hit comedy sensation in Chicago. To show his gratitude, he raised money to found the St. Jude Children's Research Hospital to help children with catastrophic illnesses such as leukemia.[236]

• Myron Cohen used to be a silk salesman who made his customers laugh, but he quit his job to become a stand-up comedian. His former boss, A.E. Wullschleger, attended one of his early appearances, and he seemed to enjoy it and laughed a lot. Afterward, Mr. Cohen asked what he thought of his act. Mr. Wullschleger looked serious for a moment, then joked, "Remember, Myron, there's always a place in my organization for a good silk salesman."[237]

• During World War II, country comedian Archie Campbell served as an enlisted man in the United States Navy under Lieutenant Sam Bailey. Both men were avid golfers, and occasionally Lieutenant Bailey would come into the enlisted men's barracks and say, "All right, men. I'm looking for a volunteer for special duty. You over there, Campbell, step out here." The "special duty" was playing a round of golf.[238]

• Tim Conway is a talented comedian who is very popular in movie roles and re-runs of *McHale's Navy* and *The Carol Burnett Show*; unfortunately, many of his own TV series have flopped. *Rango* and *The Tim Conway Comedy Hour* each lasted only 13 weeks and other shows starring Mr. Conway lasted for only half of one season. After this series of flops, Mr. Conway got new license plates for his car: "13 WKS."[239]

• Before becoming an entertainer, Whoopi Goldberg worked in a mortuary, where she dressed the hair of corpses. To do this particular job, she pretended that the corpses were just very large dolls. Later, she joked that dressing the hair of the corpses was better than dressing the hair of the living because the corpses never complained about how Ms. Goldberg made them look.[240]

• African-American entertainer George Kirby broke into show business by way of bartending. At DeLisa's in Chicago, he used to entertain customers with jokes and impressions. Mike DeLisa noticed that the customers always sat at the end of the bar where Mr. Kirby was working, so he told Mr. Kirby to put together seven minutes of material for the stage. Mr. Kirby was so successful that he appeared on stage at DeLisa's for the next five years.[241]

• Lou Costello preferred playing cards to making movies. Often, he would sit in his dressing room playing cards instead of coming out to perform his scenes. Sometimes, assistant director Howard Christie, who had played football at the University of California, would pick up Mr. Costello and carry him from the card game to the movie set.[242]

• While working in a law office, performance artist Lisa Kron wore socks instead of pantyhose, a dress code violation which made the other employees feel uneasy. However, Ms. Kron was able to disregard the dress code by telling her boss, "If I have to wear pantyhose to work every day, my yeast infection will be on your head."[243]

• Eddie Cantor was a frenetic comedian in the Ziegfeld Follies for several years, and he was known for his large "banjo" eyes, generosity to charities, and energy on stage. One of his jokes was to run onto stage, bounce around, and tell the audience, "I've just bought a secondhand watch, and this is the only way I can keep it running."[244]

• Groucho Marx was in a fancy department store when he saw a snobbish rich woman mistreating a saleslady and carrying a dog, so Groucho walked up to the rich woman and asked, "How much for the dog, miss?" She haughtily informed him that the dog was not for sale. "I'm sorry," Groucho replied, "I thought you were a salesgirl."[245]

• To make money when he was growing up, comedian Joe E. Brown used to shine shoes. However, one day he had to apologize and turn down a chance to shine a man's shoes for money. The man's shoes were tan and Joe E. Brown was so poverty-stricken that he had only one can of shoe polish—black.[246]

• Comedians and comic actors need confidence to do their jobs, but they recognize that this confidence may be misinterpreted as arrogance. Belfast, Ireland, comic Leila Webster was once asked, "What is it about a comic character that makes it funny?" She replied, "This may sound really dreadful—me."[247]

• As a boy and as a young man, Will Rogers constantly practiced his roping. While at home, he roped calves. While at school, he roped girls. Eventually, he performed his trick roping—and comedy—for audiences attending the Ziegfeld Follies.[248]

• When comedian Jonathan Winters quit his job at a television station in Columbus, Ohio, and announced that he was going to New York, people asked him, "Who do you know in New York?" Mr. Winters replied, "King Kong."[249]

Yom Kippur

• Jack Benny took pride in his Jewish heritage, although his brand of comedy seldom made his Jewishness evident. Once, he prepared for a program to be broadcast live just before Yom Kippur, which would begin at sundown. In LA, where the program originated, the program would end before sundown, but Mr. Benny realized that back East, the sun would have already set, and people might think that he was working on Yom Kippur and thus desecrating the holy day. Someone pointed out that the Jews would be in synagogue and so would not even see the program, but Mr. Benny replied, "I wasn't thinking of the Jews. I wouldn't like the Gentiles to think I didn't respect my religion."[250]

Appendix A: Bibliography

Ace, Goodman. *The Book of Little Knowledge*. New York: Simon and Schuster, 1955.

Adams, Joey. *The God Bit*. Boston, MA: G.K. Hall & Co., 1975.

Adler, Bill. *The Letterman Wit: His Life and Humor*. New York: Carroll & Graf Publishers, Inc., 1994.

Adler, Bill, and Bruce Cassiday. *The World of Jay Leno: His Humor and His Life*. New York: Carol Publishing Group, 1992.

Allen, Steve. *More Funny People*. New York: Stein and Day, Publishers, 1982.

Banks, Morwenna, and Amanda Swift. *The Joke's on Us: Women in Comedy from Music Hall to the Present Day*. London: Pandora Press, 1987.

Benchley, Nathaniel. *Robert Benchley*. New York: McGraw-Hill Book Company, Inc., 1955.

Berger, Phil. *The Last Laugh: The World of the Stand-Up Comics*. New York: William Morris and Co., Inc., 1975.

Bernhard, Sandra. *Confessions of a Pretty Lady*. New York: Harper & Row, Publishers, 1988.

Borns, Betsy. *Comic Lives: Inside the World of American Stand-Up Comedy*. New York: Simon and Schuster, Inc., 1987.

Brown, Jared. *Zero Mostel: A Biography*. New York: Atheneum, 1989.

Brown, Joe E. *Laughter is a Wonderful Thing*. As told to Ralph Hancock. New York: A.S. Barnes and Co., 1956.

Bryan III, J. *Merry Gentlemen (and One Lady)*. New York: Atheneum, 1985.

Burns, George. *All My Best Friends*. Written with David Fisher. New York: Putnam Publishing Group, 1989.

Burns, George. *Gracie: A Love Story*. New York: G.P. Putnam's Sons, 1988.

Campbell, Archie. *Archie Campbell: An Autobiography*. With Ben Bryd. Memphis, TN: Memphis State University Press, 1981.

Cantor, Eddie. *My Life is in Your Hands*. As told to David Freedman. New York and London: Harper and Brothers, Publishers, 1928.

Cantor, Eddie. *Take My Life*. Written with Jane Kesner Ardmore. Garden City, NY: Doubleday, 1957.

Caper, William. *Whoopi Goldberg: Comedian and Movie Star*. Springfield, NJ: Enslow Publications, Inc., 1999.

Carter, Judy. *The Homo Handbook*. New York: Fireside Books, 1996.

Carter, Judy. *Stand-Up Comedy: The Book*. New York: Dell Publishing, 1989.

Cartwright, Nancy. *My Life as a 10-Year-Old Boy*. New York: Hyperion, 2000.

Chapman, Graham. *Graham Crackers*. Compiled by Jim Yoakum. Franklin Lakes, NJ: Career Press, Inc., 1997.

Cho, Margaret. *I'm the One That I Want*. New York: Ballantine Books, 2001.

Claxton, William, photographer. *Laugh: Portraits of the Greatest Comedians and the Funny Stories They Tell Each Other*. Introduction by John Lithgow; conceived and produced by Andy Gould and Kathleen Bywater; text edited by Mike Thomas. New York: William Morrow, 1999.

Clemens, Cyril, editor. *Mark Twain Anecdotes*. Webster Groves, MO: Mark Twain Society, 1929.

Clinton, Kate. *Don't Get Me Started*. New York: Ballantine Books, 1998.

Clower, Jerry. *Let the Hammer Down!* With Gerry Wood. Waco, TX: Word Books, Publisher, 1979.

Clower, Jerry. *Life Everlaughter: The Heart and Humor of Jerry Clower*. Nashville, TN: Rutledge Hill Press, 1987.

Cohen, Myron. *Laughing Out Loud*. New York: The Citadel Press, 1958.

Collier, Denise, and Kathleen Beckett. *Spare Ribs: Women in the Humor Biz*. New York: St. Martin's Press, 1980.

David, Jay. *The Life and Humor of Robin Williams*. New York: William Morrow and Company, Inc., 1999.

DeGeneres, Ellen. *My Point ... And I Do Have One*. New York: Bantam Books, 1995.

Denver, Bob. *Gilligan, Maynard and Me*. New York: Carol Publishing Group, 1993.

Edelson, Edward. *Funny Men of the Movies*. New York: Pocket Books, 1976.

Epstein, Lawrence J. *A Treasury of Jewish Anecdotes*. Northvale, NJ: Jason Aronson, Inc., 1989.

Feinberg, Morris "Moe." *Larry: The Stooge in the Middle*. With G.P. Skratz. San Francisco, CA: Last Gasp of San Francisco, 1984.

Feran, Tom, and R.D. Heldenfels. *Ghoulardi: Inside Cleveland TV's Wildest Ride*. Cleveland, OH: Gray & Company, Publishers, 1997.

Forwood, Margaret. *The Real Benny Hill*. London: Robson Books, 1992.

Foxx, Redd, and Norma Miller. *The Redd Foxx Encyclopedia of Black Humor*. Pasadena, CA: Ward Ritchie Press, 1977.

Frank, Rusty E. *Tap! The Greatest Tap Dance Stars and Their Stories, 1900-1955*. New York: William Morrow and Company, Inc., 1990.

Franklin, Joe. *Joe Franklin's Encyclopedia of Comedians*. Secaucus, NJ: The Citadel Press, 1979.

Gallo, Hank. *Comedy Explosion: A New Generation*. Photographs by Ed Edahl. New York: Thunder's Mouth Press, 1991.

Green, Joey. *The Get Smart Handbook*. New York: Collier Books, 1993.

Gregory, Dick. *Nigger: An Autobiography*. With Robert Lipsyte. New York: Dutton, 1964.

Guttmacher, Peter. *Legendary Comedies*. New York: MetroBooks, 1996.

Halliwell, Leslie. *The Filmgoer's Book of Quotes*. New Rochelle, NY: Arlington House Publishers, 1973.

Hope, Bob. *The Road to Hollywood: My Forty-Year Love Affair With the Movies*. With Bob Thomas. Garden City, NY: Doubleday & Company, Inc., 1977.

Horowitz, Susan. *Queens of Comedy*. Australia: Gordon and Breach Publishers, 1997.

Howe, James. *Carol Burnett: The Sound of Laughter*. New York: Viking Kestrel, 1987.

Javna, John. *The Best of TV Sitcoms*. New York: Harmony Books, 1988.

Jewell, Geri. *Geri*. With Stewart Weiner. New York: William Morrow and Co., Inc., 1984.

Johnson, Russell, and Steve Cox. *Here on Gilligan's Isle*. New York: HarperCollins Publishers, Inc., 1993.

Kallen, Stuart A. *Great Male Comedians*. San Diego, CA: Lucent Books, 2001.

Katkov, Norman. *The Fabulous Fanny*. New York: Alfred A. Knopf, 1953.

Laffey, Bruce. *Beatrice Lillie: The Funniest Woman in the World*. New York: Wynwood Press, 1989.

Leno, Jay. *Leading With My Chin*. With Bill Zehme. New York: HarperCollins Publishers, Inc., 1996.

Leonard, Sheldon. *And the Show Goes On: Broadway and Hollywood Adventures*. New York: Limelight, 1994.

Levant, Oscar. *A Smattering of Ignorance*. New York: Doubleday, Doran, and Co., 1940.

Levenson, Sam. *In One Era and Out the Other*. New York: Simon and Schuster, 1973.

Linkletter, Art. *I Wish I'd Said That! My Favorite Ad-Libs of All Time*. Garden City, NY: Doubleday & Co., Inc., 1968.

Malone, Mary. *Will Rogers: Cowboy Philosopher*. Springfield, NJ: Enslow Publications, Inc., 1996.

Maltin, Leonard. *The Great Movie Comedians: From Charlie Chaplin to Woody Allen*. New York: Crown Publishers, Inc., 1978.

Maltin, Leonard. *Movie Comedy Teams*. New York: The New American Library, Inc., 1970.

Manchel, Frank. *The Rise of Film Comedy*. New York: Franklin Watts, Inc., 1973.

Marx, Arthur. *Life With Groucho*. New York: Simon and Schuster, 1954.

Marx, Arthur. *Son of Groucho*. New York: David McKay Company, Inc., 1972.

Marx, Groucho. *Confessions of a Mangy Lover*. New York: Da Capo Press, 1997.

Marx, Groucho. *Groucho and Me*. New York: Bernard Geis Associates, 1959.

Marx, Samuel. *Broadway Portraits*. New York: Donald Flamm, Inc., 1929.

McCabe, John. *Mr. Laurel and Mr. Hardy*. With a foreword by Dick Van Dyke. New York: Grosset and Dunlap, 1966.

Meadows, Audrey. *Love, Alice: My Life as a Honeymooner*. With Joe Daley. New York: Crown Publishers, Inc., 1994.

Meyer, Miriam Weiss, project editor. *Top Picks: People*. Pleasantville, NY: Reader's Digest Educational Division, 1977.

Miller, Norma. *Swingin' at the Savoy*. With Evette Jensen. Philadelphia, PA: Temple University Press, 1996.

Milligan, Spike. *Adolf Hitler: My Part in His Downfall*. London: Michael Joseph Limited, 1971.

Morgan, David. *Monty Python Speaks*. New York: Avon Books. Inc., 1999.

Morgan, Henry. *Here's Morgan!* New York: Barricade Books, Inc., 1994.

Morton, Robert, editor. *Stand-up Comedians on Television*. New York: Harry N. Abrams, Inc. [in association with] The Museum of Television & Radio, 1996.

Mostel, Kate, and Madeline Gilford. *170 Years of Show Business*. With Jack Gilford and Zero Mostel. New York: Random House, 1978.

Mullen, Tom. *Middle Age and Other Mixed Blessings*. Tarrytown, New York: Fleming H. Revell Company, 1991.

Nicholson, Frank Ernest. *Favorite Jokes of Famous People*. New York: E.P. Dutton & Co., Inc., 1928.

Orleans, Ellen. *The Inflatable Butch*. Los Angeles: Alyson Books, 2001.

Orleans, Ellen. *Who Cares If It's a Choice?* Bala Cynwyd, PA: Laugh Lines Press, 1994.

Phillips, Julien. *Stars of the Ziegfeld Follies*. Minneapolis, MN: Lerner Publications Company, 1972.

Rosten, Leo. *People I Have Loved, Known or Admired*. New York: McGraw-Hill Book Company, 1970.

Rudner, Rita. *Naked Beneath My Clothes*. New York: Viking Penguin, 1992.

Rudner, Rita. *Rita Rudner's Guide to Men*. New York: Viking Penguin, 1994.

Russell, Anna. *I'm Not Making This Up, You Know: The Autobiography of the Queen of Musical Parody*. New York: The Continuum Publishing Company, 1985.

Russell, Mark, editor. *Out of Character*. New York: Bantam Books, 1997.

Samra, Cal and Rose, editors. *Holy Hilarity*. Colorado Springs, CO: WaterBrook Press, 1999.

Sankey, Jay. *Zen and the Art of Stand-Up Comedy*. New York: Routledge/Theatre Arts Books, 1998.

Silverman, Stephen M. *Funny Ladies: The Women Who Make Us Laugh*. New York: Harry N. Abrams, Inc., 1999.

Slide, Anthony. *Eccentrics of Comedy*. Lanham, MD, and London: The Scarecrow Press, Inc., 1998.

Smith, Bob. *Openly Bob*. New York: William Morrow and Company, Inc., 1997.

Smith, Bob. *Way to Go, Smith!* New York: HarperCollins Publishers, Inc., 1999.

Smith, H. Allen. *Buskin' With H. Allen Smith*. New York: Trident Press, 1968.

Smith, H. Allen. *The Compleat Practical Joker*. Garden City, NY: Doubleday and Company, Inc., 1953.

Smith, Ron. *Comic Support*. New York: Carol Publishing Group, 1993.

Snead, Sam. *The Game I Love: Wisdom, Insight, and Instruction from Golf's Greatest Player*. With Fran Pirozzolo. New York: Ballantine Books, 1997.

Sorensen, Jeff. *Bob Newhart*. New York: St. Martin's Press, 1988.

Stebbins, Robert A. *The Laugh-Makers*. Montreal & Kingston, Canada: McGill-Queen's University Press, 1990.

Stone, Laurie. *Laughing in the Dark: A Decade of Subversive Comedy*. Hopewell, NJ: The Ecco Press, 1997.

Sweed, Ron "The Ghoul," and Mike Olszewski. *The Ghoul Scrapbook*. Cleveland, OH: Gray and Company, Publishers, 1998.

Taylor, Glenhall. *Before Television: The Radio Years*. New York: A.S. Barnes and Company, 1979.

Taylor, Robert Lewis. *W.C. Fields: His Follies and Fortunes*. Garden City, NY: Doubleday and Company, Inc., 1949.

Terry-Thomas, and Terry Daum. *Terry-Thomas ... Tells Tales*. London: Robson Books, 1990.

Thomas, Bob. *Bud & Lou: The Abbott and Costello Story*. Philadelphia, PA: J.B. Lippincott Company, 1977.

Took, Barry. *Comedy Greats: A Celebration of Comic Genius Past and Present*. Wellingborough, Northamptonshire, England: Equation, 1989.

Troy, Con. *Laugh with Hugh Troy, World's Greatest Practical Joker*. Wyomissing, PA: Trojan Books, 1983.

Tully, Jim. *A Dozen and One*. Hollywood, CA: Murray & Gee, Inc., Publishers, 1943.

Ullman, Tracey. *Tracey Takes On*. New York: Hyperion, 1998.

Unterbrink, Mary. *Funny Women: American Comediennes, 1860-1985*. Jefferson, NC: McFarland and Co., Inc., Publishers, 1987.

Warren, Roz, editor. *Revolutionary Laughter: The World of Women Comics.* Freedom, CA: The Crossing Press, 1995.

Weatherby, W.J. *Jackie Gleason: An Intimate Portrait.* New York: Berkley Books, 1992.

Weissman, Ginny, and Coyne Steven Sanders. *The Dick Van Dyke Show.* New York: St. Martin's Press, 1993.

Wilde, Larry. *The Great Comedians.* Secaucus, NJ: The Citadel Press, 1968.

Wilde, Larry. *How the Great Comedy Writers Create Laughter.* Chicago, IL: Nelson-Hall, Inc., 1976.

Williams, John A., and Dennis A. Williams. *If I Stop I'll Die: The Comedy and Tragedy of Richard Pryor.* New York: Thunder's Mouth Press, 1991.

Woog, Adam. *Magicians and Illusionists.* San Diego, CA: Lucent Books, 2000.

Young, Alan, and Bill Burt. *Mr. Ed and Me.* New York: St. Martin's Press, 1994.

Youngman, Henny. *Take My Life, Please!* With Neal Karlen. New York: William Morris and Company, Inc., 1991.

Zimmerman, Paul D., and Burt Goldblatt. *The Marx Brothers at the Movies.* New York: G.P. Putnam's Sons, 1968.

Zolotow, Maurice. *No People Like Show People.* New York: Random House, 1951.

Appendix B: About the Author

It was a dark and stormy night. Suddenly a cry rang out, and on a hot summer night in 1954, Josephine, wife of Carl Bruce, gave birth to a boy—me. Unfortunately, this young married couple allowed Reuben Saturday, Josephine's brother, to name their first-born. Reuben, aka "The Joker," decided that Bruce was a nice name, so he decided to name me Bruce Bruce. I have gone by my middle name—David—ever since.

Being named Bruce David Bruce hasn't been all bad. Bank tellers remember me very quickly, so I don't often have to show an ID. It can be fun in charades, also. When I was a counselor as a teenager at Camp Echoing Hills in Warsaw, Ohio, a fellow counselor gave the signs for "sounds like" and "two words," then she pointed to a bruise on her leg twice. Bruise Bruise? Oh yeah, Bruce Bruce is the answer!

Uncle Reuben, by the way, gave me a haircut when I was in kindergarten. He cut my hair short and shaved a small bald spot on the back of my head. My mother wouldn't let me go to school until the bald spot grew out again.

Of all my brothers and sisters (six in all), I am the only transplant to Athens, Ohio. I was born in Newark, Ohio, and have lived all around Southeastern Ohio. However, I moved to Athens to go to Ohio University and have never left.

At Ohio U, I never could make up my mind whether to major in English or Philosophy, so I got a bachelor's degree with a double major in both areas, then I added a Master of Arts degree in English and a Master of Arts degree in Philosophy. Yes, I have my MAMA degree.

Currently, and for a long time to come (I eat fruits and veggies), I am spending my retirement writing books such as *Nadia Comaneci: Perfect 10*, *The Funniest People in Comedy*, *Homer's* Iliad: *A Retelling in Prose*, and *William Shakespeare's* Hamlet: *A Retelling in Prose*.

If all goes well, I will publish one or two books a year for the rest of my life. (On the other hand, a good way to make God laugh is to tell Her your plans.)

By the way, my sister Brenda Kennedy writes romances such as *A New Beginning* and *Shattered Dreams*.

Appendix C: Some Books by David Bruce

Anecdote Collections

250 Anecdotes About Opera

250 Anecdotes About Religion

250 Anecdotes About Religion: Volume 2

250 Music Anecdotes

Be a Work of Art: 250 Anecdotes and Stories

The Coolest People in Art: 250 Anecdotes

The Coolest People in the Arts: 250 Anecdotes

The Coolest People in Books: 250 Anecdotes

The Coolest People in Comedy: 250 Anecdotes

Create, Then Take a Break: 250 Anecdotes

Don't Fear the Reaper: 250 Anecdotes

The Funniest People in Art: 250 Anecdotes

The Funniest People in Books: 250 Anecdotes

The Funniest People in Books, Volume 2: 250 Anecdotes

The Funniest People in Books, Volume 3: 250 Anecdotes

The Funniest People in Comedy: 250 Anecdotes

The Funniest People in Dance: 250 Anecdotes

The Funniest People in Families: 250 Anecdotes

The Funniest People in Families, Volume 2: 250 Anecdotes

The Funniest People in Families, Volume 3: 250 Anecdotes

The Funniest People in Families, Volume 4: 250 Anecdotes

The Funniest People in Families, Volume 5: 250 Anecdotes

The Funniest People in Families, Volume 6: 250 Anecdotes

The Funniest People in Movies: 250 Anecdotes

The Funniest People in Music: 250 Anecdotes

The Funniest People in Music, Volume 2: 250 Anecdotes

The Funniest People in Music, Volume 3: 250 Anecdotes

The Funniest People in Neighborhoods: 250 Anecdotes

The Funniest People in Relationships: 250 Anecdotes

The Funniest People in Sports: 250 Anecdotes

The Funniest People in Sports, Volume 2: 250 Anecdotes

The Funniest People in Television and Radio: 250 Anecdotes

The Funniest People in Theater: 250 Anecdotes

The Funniest People Who Live Life: 250 Anecdotes

The Funniest People Who Live Life, Volume 2: 250 Anecdotes

The Kindest People Who Do Good Deeds, Volume 1: 250 Anecdotes

The Kindest People Who Do Good Deeds, Volume 2: 250 Anecdotes

Maximum Cool: 250 Anecdotes

The Most Interesting People in Movies: 250 Anecdotes

The Most Interesting People in Politics and History: 250 Anecdotes

The Most Interesting People in Politics and History, Volume 2: 250 Anecdotes

The Most Interesting People in Politics and History, Volume 3: 250 Anecdotes

The Most Interesting People in Religion: 250 Anecdotes

The Most Interesting People in Sports: 250 Anecdotes

The Most Interesting People Who Live Life: 250 Anecdotes

The Most Interesting People Who Live Life, Volume 2: 250 Anecdotes

Reality is Fabulous: 250 Anecdotes and Stories

Resist Psychic Death: 250 Anecdotes

Seize the Day: 250 Anecdotes and Stories

[1] Source: James Howe, *Carol Burnett: The Sound of Laughter*, pp. 15-16.

[2] Source: Ginny Weissman and Coyne Steven Sanders, *The Dick Van Dyke Show*, pp. 48-49.

[3] Source: Ron "The Ghoul" Sweed, and Mike Olszewski, *The Ghoul Scrapbook*, p. 112.

[4] Source: John Javna, *The Best of TV Sitcoms*, p. 12.

[5] Source: Henry Morgan, *Here's Morgan!*, p. 280.

[6] Source: Larry Wilde, *The Great Comedians*, p. 36.

[7] Source: Morris "Moe" Feinberg, *Larry: The Stooge in the Middle*, p. 75.

[8] Source: Morwenna Banks and Amanda Swift, *The Joke's on Us*, p. 14.

[9] Source: Nathaniel Benchley, *Robert Benchley*, p. 245.

[10] Source: Bruce Laffey, *Beatrice Lillie*, p. 213.

[11] Source: Robert A. Stebbins, *The Laugh-Makers*, p. 92.

[12] Source: Jim Tully, *A Dozen and One*, p. 118.

[13] Source: George Burns, *Gracie: A Love Story*, pp. 184ff.

[14] Source: Ron "The Ghoul" Sweed and Mike Olszewski, *The Ghoul Scrapbook*, p. 21.

[15] Source: an A&E *Biography* program featuring Mark Twain.

[16] Source: Peter Guttmacher, *Legendary Comedies*, p. 42.

[17] Source: Anthony Slide, *Eccentrics of Comedy*, p. 27.

[18] Source: Edward Edelson, *Funny Men of the Movies*, pp. 77, 80, 82.

[19] Source: H. Allen Smith, *Buskin' With H. Allen Smith*, pp. 167-168.

[20] Source: Joey Adams, *The God Bit*, pp. 33-34.

[21] Source: H. Allen Smith, *Buskin' With H. Allen Smith*, p. 173.

[22] Source: David Morgan, *Monty Python Speaks*, p. 219.

[23] Source: Judy Carter, *The Homo Handbook*, p. 151.

[24] Source: Denise Collier and Kathleen Beckett, *Spare Ribs*, p. 127.

[25] Source: Con Troy, *Laugh with Hugh Troy*, pp. 22-24.

[26] Source: Bob Denver, *Gilligan, Maynard and Me*, p. 181.

[27] Source: Leonard Maltin, *Movie Comedy Teams*, p. 239.

[28] Source: Alan Young, *Mr. Ed and Me*, p. 31.

[29] Source: Tom Mullen, *Middle Age and Other Mixed Blessings*, pp. 30-31.

[30] Source: Bob Smith, *Openly Bob*, p. 87.

[31] Source: Nancy Cartwright, *My Life as a 10-Year-Old Boy*, p. 25.

[32] Source: Arthur Marx, *Life With Groucho*, pp. 81-82. Groucho actually said "Pyorrhea," which is a form of gum disease.

[33] Source: Judy Carter, *Stand-Up Comedy: The Book*, p. 155.

[34] Source: Robert Morton, editor, *Stand-up Comedians on Television*, p. 129.

[35] Source: Laurie Stone, *Laughing in the Dark*, pp. 135-136.

[36] Source: Betsy Borns, *Comic Lives*, p. 270.

[37] Source: Mary Unterbrink, *Funny Women*, p. 89.

[38] Source: Eddie Cantor, *Take My Life*, p. 60.

[39] Source: Sandra Bernhard, *Confessions of a Pretty Lady*, pp. 27-28.

[40] Source: Frank Ernest Nicholson, *Favorite Jokes of Famous People*, p. 113.

[41] Source: Robert Morton, editor, *Stand-up Comedians on Television*, p. 77.

[42] Source: an A&E *Biography* program featuring Jerry Lewis.

[43] Source: Cyril Clemens, editor, *Mark Twain Anecdotes*, pp. 3-4.

[44] Source: Margaret Cho, *I'm the One That I Want*, pp. 29-30.

[45] Source: Groucho Marx, *Groucho and Me*, pp. 336-337.

[46] Source: Eddie Cantor, *My Life is in Your Hands*, p. 36.

[47] Source: Sandra Bernhard, *Confessions of a Pretty Lady*, p. 28.

[48] Source: Tracey Ullman, *Tracey Takes On*, p. 111.

[49] Source: John A. Williams and Dennis A. Williams, *If I Stop I'll Die*, p. 31.

[50] Source: Bruce Laffey, *Beatrice Lillie*, p. 200.

[51] Source: an A&E *Biography* program featuring Jack Benny.

[52] Source: Bob Thomas, *Bud & Lou: The Abbott & Costello Story*, p. 148.

[53] Source: Jay Sankey, *Zen and the Art of Stand-Up Comedy*, p. 69.

[54] Source: Denise Collier and Kathleen Beckett, *Spare Ribs*, p. 48.

[55] Source: Leo Rosten, *People I Have Loved, Known or Admired*, p. 65.

[56] Source: James Howe, *Carol Burnett: The Sound of Laughter*, p. 5.

[57] Source: Stephen M. Silverman, *Funny Ladies*, p. 34.

[58] Source: Robert Lewis Taylor, *W.C. Fields: His Follies and Fortunes*, pp. 150-151.

[59] Source: Jeff Sorensen, *Bob Newhart*, p. 71.

[60] Source: Julien Phillips, *Stars of the Ziegfeld Follies*, p. 45.

[61] Source: Joe Franklin, *Joe Franklin's Encyclopedia of Comedians*, p. 160.

[62] Source: Margaret Forwood, *The Real Benny Hill*, p. 157.

[63] Source: Anthony Slide, *Eccentrics of Comedy*, p. 30.

[64] Source: Terry-Thomas, *Terry-Thomas Tells Tales*, p. 123.

[65] Source: Paul D. Zimmerman and Burt Goldblatt, *The Marx Brothers at the Movies*, p. 66.

[66] Source: Leonard Maltin, *The Great Movie Comedians*, p. 36.

[67] Source: Spike Milligan, *Adolf Hitler: My Part in His Downfall*, p. 62.

[68] Source: Henry Morgan, *Here's Morgan!*, pp. 73-74.

[69] Source: Groucho Marx, *Confessions of a Mangy Lover*, pp. 111-112.

[70] Source: Stephen M. Silverman, *Funny Ladies*, p. 23.

[71] Source: Frank Manchel, *The Rise of Film Comedy*, p. 9.

[72] Source: Bob Hope, *The Road to Hollywood*, p. 41.

[73] Source: David Morgan, *Monty Python Speaks*, p. 93.

[74] Source: Cal and Rose Samra, *Holy Hilarity*, p. 86.

[75] Source: Geri Jewell, *Geri*, pp. 187, 201-203.

[76] Source: Joe E. Brown, *Laughter is a Wonderful Thing*, pp. 258-259.

[77] Source: Eddie Cantor, *Take My Life*, p. 141.

[78] Source: Bob Smith, *Way to Go, Smith!*, pp. 202-203.

[79] Source: Kate Clinton, *Don't Get Me Started*, pp. 82-83.

[80] Source: Jay David, *The Life and Humor of Robin Williams*, p. 8.

[81] Source: Arthur Marx, *Life With Groucho*, p. 55.

[82] Source: Frank Ernest Nicholson, *Favorite Jokes of Famous People*, pp. 29-30.

[83] Source: Bill Adler and Bruce Cassiday, *The World of Jay Leno: His Humor and His Life*, p. 129.

[84] Source: Phil Berger, *The Last Laugh*, pp. 210-211.

[85] Source: Larry Wilde, *How the Great Comedy Writers Create Laughter*, p. 132.

[86] Source: Sam Levenson, *In One Era and Out the Other*, p. 66.

[87] Source: Mark Russell, editor, *Out of Character*, p. 221.

[88] Source: Susan Horowitz, *Queens of Comedy*, p. 94.

[89] Source: Steve Allen, *More Funny People*, p. 263.

[90] Source: Dick Gregory, *Nigger*, p. 89.

[91] Source: Samuel Marx, *Broadway Portraits*, p. 46.

[92] Source: Jay Leno, *Leading With My Chin*, pp. 80-81.

[93] Source: Art Linkletter, *I Wish I'd Said That!*, p. 24.

[94] Source: Graham Chapman, *Graham Crackers*, p. 73.

[95] Source: Mary Malone, *Will Rogers: Cowboy Philosopher*, p. 50.

[96] Source: an A&E *Biography* program featuring George Burns.

[97] Source: Ellen Orleans, *Who Cares If It's a Choice?*, p. 69.

[98] Source: Laurie Stone, *Laughing in the Dark*, p. 184.

[99] Source: Ellen Orleans, *The Inflatable Butch*, p. 44.

[100] Source: Judy Carter, *The Homo Handbook*, pp. 13-14.

[101] Source: Ellen Orleans, *Who Cares If It's a Choice?*, p. 58.

[102] Source: Archie Campbell, *Archie Campbell: An Autobiography*, pp. 64-65.

[103] Source: Myron Cohen, *Laughing Out Loud*, p. 177.

[104] Source: Margaret Cho, *I'm the One That I Want*, pp. 207-208.

[105] Source: Norman Katkov, *The Fabulous Fanny*, pp. 115, 136.

[106] Source: Paul D. Zimmerman and Burt Goldblatt, *The Marx Brothers at the Movies*, pp. 185-186.

[107] Source: Rita Rudner, *Naked Beneath My Clothes*, pp. 52-53.

[108] Source: Jared Brown, *Zero Mostel: A Biography*, p. 55.

[109] Source: Jim Tully, *A Dozen and One*, p. 25.

[110] Source: Goodman Ace, *The Book of Little Knowledge*, p. 105.

[111] Source: Glenhall Taylor, *Before Television*, pp. 148-149.

[112] Source: Russell Johnson and Steve Cox, *Here on Gilligan's Isle*, p. 53.

[113] Source: Kate Mostel and Madeline Gilford, *170 Years of Show Business*, p. 156.

[114] Source: Rita Rudner, *Rita Rudner's Guide to Men*, No. 191.

[115] Source: George Burns, *Gracie: A Love Story*, p. 27.

[116] Source: Leslie Halliwell, *The Filmgoer's Book of Quotes*, p. 209.

[117] Source: Norma Miller, *Swingin' at the Savoy*, p. 222.

[118] Source: an A&E *Biography* program featuring Ernie Kovacs.

[119] Source: Spike Milligan, *Adolf Hitler: My Part in His Downfall*, p. 70.

[120] Source: Jay David, *The Life and Humor of Robin Williams*, p. 179.

[121] Source: George Burns, *All My Best Friends*, p. 306.

[122] Source: Bill Adler, *The Letterman Wit: His Life and Humor*, p. 41.

[123] Source: Joey Adams, *The God Bit*, pp. 330-331.

[124] Source: an A&E *Biography* program featuring Joan Rivers.

[125] Source: Groucho Marx, *Groucho and Me*, p. 327.

[126] Source: Robert Lewis Taylor, *W.C. Fields: His Follies and Fortunes*, p. 105.

[127] Source: an A&E *Biography* program featuring Tim Allen.

[128] Source: Tom Mullen, *Middle Age and Other Mixed Blessings*, p. 60.

[129] Source: Cal and Rose Samra, *Holy Hilarity*, pp. 93-94.

[130] Source: Roz Warren, editor, *Revolutionary Laughter*, p. 108.

[131] Source: Maurice Zolotow, *No People Like Show People*, p. 158.

[132] Source: Glenhall Taylor, *Before Television*, pp. 155-156.

[133] Source: Leonard Maltin, *The Great Movie Comedians*, pp. 166-67.

[134] Source: Rusty E. Frank, *Tap!*, p. 148.

[135] Source: Frank Manchel, *The Rise of Film Comedy*, p. 26.

[136] Source: Jerry Clower, *Let the Hammer Down!*, pp. 36-37.

[137] Source: Groucho Marx, *Confessions of a Mangy Lover*, pp. 176-177.

[138] Source: Ron Smith, *Comic Support*, p. 49.

[139] Source: Rita Rudner, *Naked Beneath My Clothes*, pp. 39-40.

[140] Source: Sam Snead, *The Game I Love*, p. 161.

[141] Source: Audrey Meadows, *Love, Alice*, p. 34.

[142] Source: Anna Russell, *I'm Not Making This Up, You Know*, p. 219.

[143] Source: Betsy Borns, *Comic Lives*, p. 42.

[144] Source: Arthur Marx, *Son of Groucho*, p. 31.

[145] Source: Bill Adler and Bruce Cassiday, *The World of Jay Leno: His Humor and His Life*, pp. 8-9.

[146] Source: John A. Williams and Dennis A. Williams, *If I Stop I'll Die*, p. 43.

[147] Source: Jared Brown, *Zero Mostel: A Biography*, p. 22.

[148] Source: Miriam Weiss Meyer, project editor, *Top Picks: People*, p. 7.

[149] Source: Judy Carter, *Stand-Up Comedy: The Book*, p. 130.

[150] Source: Larry Wilde, *How the Great Comedy Writers Create Laughter*, p. 114.

[151] Source: Graham Chapman, *Graham Crackers*, p. 127.

[152] Source: Adam Woog, *Magicians and Illusionists*, pp. 96, 98.

[153] Source: Phil Berger, *The Last Laugh*, pp. 363-364.

[154] Source: Norman Katkov, *The Fabulous Fanny*, p. 165.

[155] Source: Art Linkletter, *I Wish I'd Said That!*, p. 98.

[156] Source: Joey Green, *The Get Smart Handbook*, pp. 27, 30.

[157] Source: Leslie Halliwell, *The Filmgoer's Book of Quotes*, Foreword.

[158] Source: Eddie Cantor, *My Life is in Your Hands*, p. 289.

[159] Source: Sam Levenson, *In One Era and Out the Other*, p. 30.

[160] Source: Morris "Moe" Feinberg, *Larry: The Stooge in the Middle*, pp. 9, 142.

[161] Source: Jerry Clower, *Life Everlaughter*, pp. 52-53.

[162] Source: Nancy Cartwright, *My Life as a 10-Year-Old Boy*, p. 76.

[163] Source: Jerry Clower, *Let the Hammer Down!*, p. 146.

[164] Source: Edward Edelson, *Funny Men of the Movies*, p. 58.

[165] Source: Anna Russell, *I'm Not Making This Up, You Know*, p. 69.

[166] Source: Terry-Thomas, *Terry-Thomas Tells Tales*, p. 123.

[167] Source: J. Bryan III, *Merry Gentlemen (and One Lady)*, p. 58.

[168] Source: Geri Jewell, *Geri*, p. 199.

[169] Source: an A&E *Biography* program featuring Jonathan Winters.

[170] Source: Arthur Marx, *Son of Groucho*, p. 39.

[171] Source: Ellen DeGeneres, *My Point ... And I Do Have One*, p. 193.

[172] Source: Bob Hope, *The Road to Hollywood*, p. 40.

[173] Source: Oscar Levant, *A Smattering of Ignorance*, pp. 57-58.

[174] Source: Roz Warren, editor, *Revolutionary Laughter*, pp. 17-18.

[175] Source: Kate Clinton, *Don't Get Me Started*, pp. 192-193.

[176] Source: William Claxton, *Laugh*, p. 61.

[177] Source: Tom Feran and R.D. Heldenfels, *Ghoulardi*, p. 64.

[178] Source: Cyril Clemens, editor, *Mark Twain Anecdotes*, p. 4.

[179] Source: Bill Adler, *The Letterman Wit: His Life and Humor*, pp. 14-15.

[180] Source: Sheldon Leonard, *And the Show Goes On*, pp. 63-64.

[181] Source: H. Allen Smith, *The Compleat Practical Joker*, p. 33.

[182] Source: Stuart A. Kallen, *Great Male Comedians*, p. 21.

[183] Source: Con Troy, *Laugh with Hugh Troy*, pp. 77-78.

[184] Source: Joe Franklin, *Joe Franklin's Encyclopedia of Comedians*, p. 69.

[185] Source: H. Allen Smith, *The Compleat Practical Joker*, p. 122.

[186] Source: Oscar Levant, *A Smattering of Ignorance*, pp. 56-57.

[187] Source: Jerry Clower, *Life Everlaughter*, p. 82.

[188] Source: Larry Wilde, *The Great Comedians*, p. 258.

[189] Source: Redd Foxx and Norma Miller, *The Redd Foxx Encyclopedia of Black Humor*, p. 166.

[190] Source: Dick Gregory, *Nigger*, p. 160.

[191] Source: Bob Smith, *Openly Bob*, p. 259.

[192] Source: Stuart A. Kallen, *Great Male Comedians*, pp. 32-33.

[193] Source: Bob Smith, *Way to Go, Smith!*, pp. 117-119.

[194] Source: Hank Gallo, *Comedy Explosion: A New Generation*, p. 92.

[195] Source: Jay Leno, *Leading With My Chin*, pp. 44-45.

[196] Source: Audrey Meadows, *Love, Alice*, p. 148.

[197] Source: Ellen Orleans, *The Inflatable Butch*, p. 47.

[198] Source: William Claxton, *Laugh*, p. 5.

[199] Source: Mary Unterbrink, *Funny Women*, p. 153.

[200] Source: Norma Miller, *Swinging' at the Savoy*, pp. 208-209.

[201] Source: W.J. Weatherby, *Jackie Gleason: An Intimate Portrait*, p. 46.

[202] Source: Ron Smith, *Comic Support*, p. 200.

[203] Source: Margaret Forwood, *The Real Benny Hill*, p. 120.

[204] Source: George Burns, *All My Best Friends*, p. 266.

[205] Source: W.J. Weatherby, *Jackie Gleason: An Intimate Portrait*, p. 132.

[206] Source: Henny Youngman, *Take My Life, Please!*, pp. 117-8.

[207] Source: Robert A. Stebbins, *The Laugh-Makers*, p. 45.

[208] Source: Peter Guttmacher, *Legendary Comedies*, p. 17.

[209] Source: Susan Horowitz, *Queens of Comedy*, p. 102.

[210] Source: Maurice Zolotow, *No People Like Show People*, pp. 106-107.

[211] Source: Jeff Sorensen, *Bob Newhart*, p. 127.

[212] Source: Barry Took, *Comedy Greats*, p. 12.

[213] Source: John McCabe, *Mr. Laurel and Mr. Hardy*, p. 187.

[214] Source: Henny Youngman, *Take My Life, Please!*, pp. 170-171.

[215] Source: Russell Johnson and Steve Cox, *Here on Gilligan's Isle*, p. 23.

[216] Source: Nathaniel Benchley, *Robert Benchley*, p. 3.

[217] Source: J. Bryan III, *Merry Gentlemen (and One Lady)*, p. 32.

[218] Source: Leo Rosten, *People I Have Loved, Known or Admired*, p. 74.

[219] Source: John McCabe, *Mr. Laurel and Mr. Hardy*. This anecdote comes from Mr. Dick Van Dyke's funeral elegy for Mr. Laurel, p. 4.

[220] Source: Ginny Weissman and Coyne Steven Sanders, *The Dick Van Dyke Show*, p. 69.

[221] Source: Sheldon Leonard, *And the Show Goes On*, p. 78.

[222] Source: Alan Young, *Mr. Ed and Me*, p. 34.

[223] Source: Bob Denver, *Gilligan, Maynard and Me*, p. 82.

[224] Source: Joey Green, *The Get Smart Handbook*, p. 4.

[225] Source: John Javna, *The Best of TV Sitcoms*, p. 120.

[226] Source: Leonard Maltin, *Movie Comedy Teams*, p. 246.

[227] Source: Barry Took, *Comedy Greats*, p. 202.

[228] Source: William Caper, *Whoopi Goldberg: Comedian and Movie Star*, pp. 30, 32.

[229] Source: Adam Woog, *Magicians and Illusionists*, p. 15.

[230] Source: Hank Gallo, *Comedy Explosion: A New Generation*, p. 33.

[231] Source: Samuel Marx, *Broadway Portraits*, p. 59.

[232] Source: Kate Mostel and Madeline Gilford, *170 Years of Show Business*, p. 108.

[233] Source: Jay Sankey, *Zen and the Art of Stand-Up Comedy*, p. 99.

[234] Source: Rusty E. Frank, *Tap!*, p. 138.

[235] Source: Tom Feran and R.D. Heldenfels, *Ghoulardi*, p. 36.

[236] Source: an A&E *Biography* program featuring Danny Thomas.

[237] Source: Myron Cohen, *Laughing Out Loud*, p. 15.

[238] Source: Archie Campbell, *Archie Campbell: An Autobiography*, pp. 79, 81.

[239] Source: Steve Allen, *More Funny People*, p. 124.

[240] Source: William Caper, *Whoopi Goldberg: Comedian and Movie Star*, p. 28.

[241] Source: Redd Foxx and Norma Miller, *The Redd Foxx Encyclopedia of Black Humor*, pp. 156, 158.

[242] Source: Bob Thomas, *Bud & Lou*, pp. 155-156.

[243] Source: Mark Russell, editor, *Out of Character*, p. 220.

[244] Source: Julien Phillips, *Stars of the Ziegfeld Follies*, p. 79.

[245] Source: Goodman Ace, *The Book of Little Knowledge*, p. 107.

[246] Source: Joe E. Brown, *Laughter is a Wonderful Thing*, p. 13.

[247] Source: Morwenna Banks and Amanda Swift, *The Joke's on Us*, p. 117.

[248] Source: Mary Malone, *Will Rogers: Cowboy Philosopher*, p. 19.

[249] Source: an A&E *Biography* program featuring Jonathan Winters.

[250] Source: Lawrence J. Epstein, *A Treasury of Jewish Anecdotes*, p. 37.